Ephesians

A 40-DAY BIBLE STUDY

"This daily devotional is something I've longed for. It is expositional, theological, and practical as it walks verse by verse through a book of the Bible in just 40 days. With such an outstanding stable of contributors, it is certain to become widely used in the days to come."

DANIEL L. AKIN,
president, Southeastern Baptist Theological Seminary, North Carolina

"I cannot think of a greater gift to the church than a biblically rooted devotional series, which spans the entire New Testament. Christians need to study the Bible, and they need to read it devotionally, prayerfully, and expecting God's power to manifest through their reading of the pages of Scripture. The Planted in the Word series—which works through the Bible book by book, chapter by chapter, and line by line—will nourish the faith of Christians in a profound way for many years to come."

R. ALBERT MOHLER,
president, The Southern Baptist Theological Seminary, Kentucky

"Let's be honest: daily Bible reading and prayer can get stale and tiresome. We need a fresh angle! The Planted in the Word volumes provide it. Seasoned scholars explain the text, relate it to Christ, apply it, and offer a sample prayer. Additional questions facilitate personal growth or group discussion. This is a treasure chest of Bible exposition, not random but rather in the flow of each biblical book. Follow these guides for a clearer grasp of Scripture, direction in living it out, and motivation for rich, Scripture-grounded communion with God."

ROBERT W. YARBROUGH,
professor of New Testament, Covenant Theological Seminary, Missouri

"As a pastor, I'm constantly seeking resources that help our congregation dive deeper into the Scriptures—reading, understanding, and living out God's Word. The Planted in the Word series delivers this in an outstanding way. The level of scholarship throughout is truly exceptional, and I have great trust and respect for each of the contributors. I'm excited to place these valuable tools in the hands of our church members, knowing they will be well-equipped to grow in their faith."

JASON DEES,
senior pastor, Christ Covenant, Atlanta, Georgia

Ephesians

A 40-DAY BIBLE STUDY

BENJAMIN L. MERKLE

Benjamin L. Merkle, Series Editor

Ephesians: A 40-Day Bible Study
Planted in the Word, edited by Benjamin L. Merkle

Lexham Press, 1313 Bay St., Bellingham, WA 98225
LexhamPress.com

Print ISBN 9781683598046
Digital ISBN 9781683598053
Library of Congress Control Number 2025941177

Lexham Editorial: Elliot Ritzema, Allisyn Ma, Abigail Stocker
Cover Design: Joshua Hunt
Typesetting: Jessi Strong

25 26 27 28 29 30 31 / US / 12 11 10 9 8 7 6 5 4 3 2 1

Contents

Series Preface

The longest book of the Bible begins by describing someone who is blessed (Ps 1:1–3). Such a person does not walk with the wicked, stand with sinners, or sit with scoffers. Instead, they delight in God's law, meditating on it day and night. They are further described as a tree that is located in an ideal setting—it is planted by streams of water. Water brings nourishment and sustenance to a tree. Without water, a tree will wither and die. But with sufficient water comes growth, causing the tree to produce its fruit. Where the tree is planted makes all the difference. If it is planted by a stream, it has a continual source of life-giving water.

God's word is the water that nourishes the soul. Without it, we spiritually wither or shrivel, and in order to continue "life as normal" we are forced to draw sustenance from other places—places that were never designed to give us what only God can. The goal of this series is to help you experience God's blessing by planting you beside the stream of God's life-giving word. Each volume consists of forty days of guided Bible study through a particular book (or books) of the New Testament. And each day's study consists of five components:

1. *Read* the passage of Scripture.

2. *Meditate* on the meaning of the text.

3. *Reflect on Christ*, since all the promises of God are "yes" and "amen" in him (2 Cor 1:20).
4. *Apply God's word* because it is alive and active, and it is what God uses to transform us into the image of his Son.
5. *Pray*, asking for God's help.

Additionally, the *Study It Further* section provides a way for you to dig deeper by examining how the Old Testament provides the background for the passage, by looking at a particular word or theme elsewhere in the New Testament, or by encouraging you to consider how the passage relates to you personally.

So, drink deeply from God's word. Let us not be like those who are influenced by the things of this world, causing us to drift farther and farther away from God (from walking, to standing, and eventually to sitting with the wicked). Instead, let us be planted in the word, drawing continual nourishment for our souls through the life-giving and fruit-producing words of the living God.

Benjamin L. Merkle
Series Editor

Introduction to Ephesians

Although Ephesians is a somewhat short letter—containing only 6 chapters and 155 verses—it has had a profound impact on the church for the past two millennia. Some have suggested that, among New Testament books, only the Gospel of John and Romans have had more influence in shaping the behavior and beliefs of Christians. But why has this short letter left such an enduring and significant imprint on the lives of believers? I think it is due to both the depth and diversity of topics revealed in this epistle. Not only does the apostle Paul unpack and explain certain topics in great detail, but he does so with a wide variety of issues. For instance, he addresses in significant depth the meaning and benefits of our union with Christ, God's sovereignty in election and salvation, the unity of the church, the various roles in marriage and the family, and the stark reality of spiritual warfare. It is no wonder that believers are drawn to this Spirit-inspired letter.

AUTHOR AND DATE

The apostle Paul twice identifies himself as the author of Ephesians (1:1; 3:1). We know Paul was imprisoned when he wrote this letter because in three places he mentions being a "prisoner" (3:1; 4:1) or being "in chains" (6:20). Although some have suggested Ephesus or Caesarea as the location of Paul's imprisonment, the most likely place is Rome, which means the date of the letter's composition is somewhere between AD 60–62. Paul spent two years in Rome under house arrest guarded by an imperial soldier (Acts 28:30). During that time, he also wrote Philippians, Colossians, and Philemon. Together, these four letters are known as the Prison Epistles.

LOCATION AND OCCASION

Paul first visited Ephesus on his second missionary journey (Acts 18:18–21). He returned to Ephesus on his third journey and ministered there for about three years (Acts 19:1). During this longer stay in Ephesus, Paul proclaimed the gospel to many Jews and gentiles, cast out demons from those possessed, witnessed the burning of expensive magic scrolls by new converts to Christianity, and survived a riot incited by some enraged followers of Artemis (Acts 19:11–41). Indeed, Ephesus was the home of the temple of Artemis—also known by the Romans as Diana—which was considered one of the wonders of the ancient world (Acts 19:35). This temple was perhaps the largest building in its day, possessing columns sixty feet high. Known as the Artemisia, this temple was not only a religious center; it also functioned as the cultural center of the city (including its primary banking institution). The goddess Artemis was a dominant fixture of Ephesian life, as she was featured on Ephesian coins, was the inspiration for the naming of one of the months and several athletic games, and was known as the guardian and protector of the city. So when people began to abandon Artemis and follow Jesus, this shift in devotion unsurprisingly caused an uproar.

RECIPIENTS

This letter is named after the recipients and the city in which they resided: "to the faithful saints in Christ Jesus *at Ephesus* (1:1). Unlike most of Paul's letters that target specific issues or crises in the churches, this letter remains more general. The church was composed of mostly, though not exclusively, gentile Christians. For example, he refers to them as "Gentiles in the flesh" and exhorts them to remember that before their conversion they "were without Christ, excluded from the citizenship of Israel, and foreigners to the covenants of promise, without hope and without God in the world" (2:11, 12). Later, he notes that his imprisonment was "on behalf of you Gentiles" (3:1), and he exhorts them to "no longer walk as the Gentiles do, in the futility of their thoughts" (4:17).

THEMES

At least three themes are prominent in Ephesians: union with Christ, the unity of the church, and the holiness of the Christian. First, Paul emphasizes our union with Christ, which results in our being chosen, redeemed, adopted, and sealed with the Spirit (1:3–14). In fact, every spiritual blessing that we receive is because we are "in Christ." Although we were dead in our sins, God gives us new life so that we are made alive, raised, and seated with Christ in the heavenly places (2:1–6). Furthermore, because we are in Christ, we are brought near to God, receiving his peace (2:13–14). It is only through Christ that we have access to the Father (2:18). And it is those who are in Christ who are joined together as a holy temple, which is a dwelling place for the Spirit of God (2:20–22).

Second, Paul emphasizes the unity of the church. That is, Jews and gentiles have unity with one another because of their common union with Christ. Through his death on the cross, Jesus has broken down the dividing wall so that the two groups have become one (2:14), creating a new humanity (2:15). Those who were once enemies have been reconciled (2:16). Consequently, all those united to Christ are now fellow citizens and fellow members of God's household (2:19). In the past, this unity of God's people was somewhat hidden (a mystery), but now in the gospel it has been revealed (3:6). Believers are called to strive to keep and protect this unity (4:1–3) since, after all, in Christ there is one body, one Spirit, one hope, one Lord, one faith, one baptism, and one God and Father of all (4:4–6).

Third, Paul emphasizes the holiness of the Christian. As believers, we are called to live worthy of our calling (4:1). We were once far from God and lived contrary to his ways (2:1–3, 12), but we must no longer live as unbelievers whose minds, understanding, and hearts are darkened, and whose actions are contrary to God's laws (4:17–19). Instead, we are to put off the old self and put on the new self, which is "created after the likeness of God in true righteousness and holiness" (4:22–25). We are to live carefully, making wise decisions (5:15) and relating to others appropriately (5:21–6:9). Finally, walking in holiness includes not only fighting against our sinful nature, it also includes battling against spiritual forces with the strength that God provides (6:10–20).

Ephesians contains both helpful theological guidance regarding how we should think and also wise practical guidance regarding how we should live. It reminds us of who we were before we put our faith in Christ and encourages us to recall all of the blessings we have in Christ. May this study of Ephesians strengthen your faith and cause your love for Christ and his people to increase.

Day 1

Ephesians 1:1–2

READ

Paul, an apostle of Christ Jesus by the will of God,
To the saints who are in Ephesus,
and are faithful in Christ Jesus:
Grace to you and peace from God our
Father and the Lord Jesus Christ.

MEDITATE

Although our modern convention is to end letters with a signature and perhaps our credentials, the ancient convention was to begin a letter by identifying the author. After identifying himself, Paul offers his credentials: he is an apostle of Christ Jesus. The term "apostle" can be used in a non-technical manner, referring to someone who was sent out as an emissary to carry a message or to deliver a material good on behalf of another. But here, Paul uses the term more technically as a designation of someone who was chosen and commissioned by Jesus himself (see 1 Cor 9:1; 15:9), a term that was reserved for the twelve apostles as those who had a unique position in the founding of the church (see Matt 10:2; Acts 1:13; 1 Cor 15:5, 7). Paul did not make himself an apostle. Rather, his apostleship is "by the will of God." In fact, at the time God called Paul to serve him in this capacity, Paul was persecuting the church and was the church's zealous enemy.

We are called saints: Most people, if they are honest, don't think of themselves as saints. This is perhaps true for Christians as well. Paul, however, identifies his readers who live in the city of Ephesus as "saints" (1:2). This term doesn't mean that they were perfect or had attained a special status via their behavior. Rather, it indicated that they were set apart as God's chosen people, and as such they were called to live according to God's standards and not those of the world.

We are called to faith: These Christians are also referred to as those who are "faithful." That is, they heard the gospel message and responded positively in faith, believing that Jesus was the promised Messiah. In addition, it could also signify their obedience to walk in accordance with the apostolic message.

We receive grace and peace: The final part of the introduction (after the identification of the author and the recipients) is the greeting. Although Paul uses this exact formula elsewhere (Rom 1:7; 1 Cor 1:3; 2 Cor 1:2; Gal 1:3; Phil 1:2; 2 Thess 1:2; and Phlm 3), it is packed full of significance and was not simply a rote formality. Paul wishes "grace" and "peace" upon his readers, two themes that are repeatedly emphasized in this letter (together occurring about twenty times). Grace is God's unmerited or, better, demerited favor. More specifically, it refers to all the benefits we receive due to God's saving act in Jesus's sacrificial death. Peace is not merely the absence of war; it is experiencing life as God intended, which includes freedom from sin. Although perfect peace will only be experienced in the new heavens and new earth, God grants us his peace even now as we align ourselves with his will.

REFLECT ON CHRIST

Paul identifies himself as an apostle of Jesus Christ (1:2). He was called by Christ. He was commissioned by Christ. He served Christ. And he belonged to Christ. His authority as an apostle came from Christ.

Paul also indicates that the twofold blessing of *grace* and *peace* comes not only from God the Father but from the Lord Jesus Christ. Such a status demonstrates that Jesus is equal to the Father as one who is the source of divine blessings. Later in Ephesians, Paul notes that the grace that believers receive is "in the Beloved" (1:6)—that is, in Christ. Furthermore, our union with Christ secures our redemption, which is in accordance with the immeasurable riches of God's grace (1:7; 2:7). The grace of spiritual gifts that believers receive is "according to the measure of Christ's gift" (4:7).

Peace also is tied to Christ in Ephesians. Christ preached peace to those who were far off and those who were near (2:17). He is our peace (2:14). Through his work on the cross for us, he has made peace by breaking down the dividing wall and by creating one new humanity (2:15). Grace and peace are found in Christ, so all those united to him by faith have access to these incredible blessings.

APPLY GOD'S WORD

Paul's calling to preach the good news to the gentiles (non-Jews) was part of God's sovereign plan. Paul did not appoint himself to this task. In fact, at the time of his calling, he was persecuting Christians, seeking to arrest those who were proclaiming that Jesus was the promised Messiah. It was God's unmerited grace and favor that turned Paul from a persecutor of Jesus to a proclaimer of Jesus. He did not receive the title "apostle" through his own merits or good works. It was a sovereign gift of God.

Later, Paul would write, "Christ Jesus came into the world to save sinners, of whom I am the foremost. But I received mercy for this reason, that in me, as the foremost, Jesus Christ might display his perfect patience as an example to those who were to believe in him for eternal life" (1 Tim 1:15–16). Although Paul may have received a unique calling as an apostle, the mercy, grace, and peace he received serve as an example for all. God did not lavish his grace on us because of something desirable in us but purely because of his love and grace which are found in Christ Jesus. Thanks be to God!

PRAY

Dear Lord, thank you that you do not leave me in my sin but that you have called me into a relationship with you through your Son, Jesus Christ. Thank you that through him I can even now experience your grace and peace in my life. And Lord, help me today to be a conduit of that grace and peace to others. Amen.

STUDY IT FURTHER

1. Read Matthew 10:1–4; Acts 1:21–26; and 1 Corinthians 15:5–10. What do these verses teach us about the calling and authority of the apostles?

2. Besides the church at Ephesus, Paul addresses several other churches as "saints" (see Rom 1:7; 1 Cor 1:2; 2 Cor 1:1; Phil 1:1; Col 1:2). Some of those churches were known for their immorality (see, for example, 1 Corinthians). How can Paul call them (and us) saints?

3. Read Philippians 4:7 and Colossians 3:15. These passages highlight the peace of God. How does the peace of God/Christ help believers?

Day 2

Ephesians 1:3–6

READ

Blessed be the God and Father of our Lord Jesus Christ, who has blessed us in Christ with every spiritual blessing in the heavenly places, even as he chose us in him before the foundation of the world, that we should be holy and blameless before him. In love he predestined us for adoption to himself as sons through Jesus Christ, according to the purpose of his will, to the praise of his glorious grace, with which he has blessed us in the Beloved.

MEDITATE

I often end a note or email to friends with the word "blessings" before I sign off. By that I am communicating to them that I am grateful for their friendship and that I desire God's favor to rest upon them. Used in this way, the word "blessing" communicates something passive—that is, something we receive. People can be a blessing to us. But ultimately, all blessings come from God (Eph 1:3; Jas 1:17), even though we often conceive of a blessing as something that is given to us or is received by us. In the beginning of Ephesians, Paul erupts with praise to God by acknowledging that God is worthy to be blessed. Because of God's great love shown to us through Jesus Christ, our natural response should be to bless or praise God. Interestingly, in the original language (Greek), this sentence beginning in verse 3 does not end until verse 14 (202 words; almost as long as this paragraph you are reading). What we might call a run-on or an abnormally long sentence is a natural, spontaneous result of contemplating the grace and mercy of God. We should bless or praise God because he blesses us in Christ Jesus. Note the emphasis on blessing: "*Blessed* be the God and Father of our Lord Jesus Christ, who has *blessed* us in Christ with every spiritual *blessing*" (emphasis added, 1:3). In verses 3–14, Paul informs us of three main reasons why we should bless God.

God chose us before the foundation of the world: The first reason relates to election: God has *chosen* us in Christ before the foundation of the world. In the Old Testament, God chose Abraham to be a blessing to the nations (Gen 12:1–3). He also chose Israel to be his treasured possession (Deut 7:6–8; 14:2). Similarly, God chose a people for himself in Christ. Our response to God's gracious election should express itself in praise to him for such blessing. We love God because he first loved and chose us (1 John 4:19).

God chose us to be holy and blameless: When God chooses someone, he chooses them for a purpose: they are to be holy and blameless—set apart for God. Just as the priests in the Old Testament were set apart as God's minsters, so Christians are set apart to be devoted to God and walk according to his statutes. He chose us so that we would be like him.

God chose us in love to be part of his family: Even more amazing is that God chose and predestined us to be included in his family—to be his children and receive all the benefits that such a privilege affords. God's choice is grounded in his love (see Eph 2:4). Our new status is even more meaningful when we realize that we were once "sons of disobedience" (2:2) and "children of wrath" (2:3), but now we can call God our Father. Again, our response to God's grand plan of redemption is to break out in praise to our gracious Creator and Redeemer. In fact, God's election was done with the purpose that his redeemed children might praise his glorious grace. In his abundant kindness, God has freely granted salvation to those who did not deserve it. Paul begins and ends this passage with blessing and praising God: "Blessed be the God and Father of our Lord Jesus Christ ... to the praise of his glorious grace" (1:3, 6). We should praise God because he graciously chose us.

REFLECT ON CHRIST

Notice that this passage focuses on the spiritual blessings that we have *in Christ*. The following phrases occur: "of our Lord Jesus Christ," "in Christ," "in him," "through Jesus Christ," and "in the Beloved." The point is that we are blessed by God because of our union with Christ. That is, we receive these blessings specifically because we believe in Christ's death, resurrection, and ascension and are united with him through faith.

The significance of being "in Christ" can hardly be overstated. Christ alone provides us access to the Father because of his finished work on the cross. The grace that the Father lavishes on us as his children comes to us because we are "in the Beloved," that is, "in Christ." Not only is Christ the recipient par excellence of the Father's love and affection (Col 1:13), but it is through his beloved Son that we receive his blessings. Although God the Father is the one we praise because of his electing grace, that grace is offered to us because the Son has faithfully secured our salvation. Because he is the Beloved, we are now beloved.

APPLY GOD'S WORD

We have much for which to praise God, but we often are distracted by the issues, pressures, and trials before us. It is good and right for us to pause and praise God for his abundant mercy. Though we were once his enemies, we are now those who have been adopted as children.

God's election has an end goal. Specifically, we are chosen by God "that we should be holy and blameless before him" (1:4; compare Col 1:22). With the privilege of election comes the responsibility of living according to God's word and God's will. Our redemption has a divine purpose. God desires not only to forgive our sins but to conform us to the image of his beloved Son (Rom 8:29–30).

God wants his children to be like him. Quoting Leviticus 11:44, Peter writes, "But as he who called you is holy, you also be holy in all your conduct, since it is written, 'You shall be holy, for I am holy' " (1 Pet 1:15–16). Later in Ephesians, Paul writes that Christ loved and died for the church so that "she might be holy and without blemish" (5:27). It is not only on the last day that we will be holy; we are to strive in the strength that God provides to comply to God's word now.

Today, we have been reminded of God's amazing grace and love that led him to choose us even though we were once his disobedient enemies. Our response to such grace is to bless God for the great salvation we possess. Because we have freely received salvation based only on Christ's work on the cross, we are to walk in joyful obedience to our loving, heavenly Father.

PRAY

Dear almighty God, I confess to you that I frequently delight in many things other than you. Through my union with Christ, give me the unswerving desire to conform to your will. I confess that without you I can do nothing, so grant me strength this day to walk in your ways. In the name of your beloved Son, Jesus Christ, amen.

STUDY IT FURTHER

1. Read Genesis 12:1–3 (God's choosing and blessing of Abraham) and Deuteronomy 7:6–8 (God's choosing of Israel). What do these verses teach us about the *basis* and *purpose* of God's choice?

2. Paul states that the election of God's people took place "before the foundation of the world" (Eph 1:4). This phrase also occurs in John 17:24 and 1 Peter 1:20. What do you think this phrase means and why does Paul mention it?

3. The term "adoption" is used only five times in the New Testament, all by Paul (Rom 8:15, 23; 9:4; Gal 4:5). In Greco-Roman culture those who were adopted were given the full status of the family and became heirs of the family's estate. How should such full and complete acceptance of God's people affect how we live today?

Day 3

Ephesians 1:7–10

READ

In him we have redemption through his blood,
the forgiveness of our trespasses, according
to the riches of his grace, which he lavished upon us,
in all wisdom and insight making known to us the mystery
of his will, according to his purpose, which he set forth in
Christ as a plan for the fullness of time, to unite
all things in him, things in heaven and things on earth.

MEDITATE

Paul's statement in Ephesians 1:7–10 has so many good nuggets of truth that it can be overwhelming. Because there is so much here, we might wonder what the main idea is. Notice how deep and meaningful some of these words are: redemption, forgiveness, grace, wisdom, insight, will, purpose, plan. Based on the structure of the larger section, however, the main point is clear: God is worthy to be praised because he *redeems* us (the second of four reasons provided in 1:3–14).

God redeems us through Christ's blood: The term "redemption" indicates release or liberation from imprisonment or captivity.

In the Old Testament, it describes both the release of slaves from bondage (Exod 21:8; Lev 25:48) and the deliverance of God's people from slavery in Egypt (Deut 7:8; 9:26; 13:5; 1 Chr 17:21). Elsewhere, Paul writes that believers have been "bought with a price" (1 Cor 6:20; 7:23) and that "Christ redeemed us from the curse of the law by becoming a curse for us" (Gal 3:13). Specifically, our redemption is secured "through his blood" (Eph 1:7)—that is, through the sacrificial death of Jesus on the cross on our behalf. The result of such redemption is "the forgiveness of our trespasses" (1:7). We deserved God's just judgment, but instead we are granted forgiveness. This indeed is reason to praise God!

God redeems us according to his lavish grace: But why would God desire to forgive a wayward and rebellious sinner? The answer is because of his grace. In verse 6 Paul spoke of God's "glorious grace," and in verse 7 he refers to the "riches of his grace." This rich grace is "lavished" (v. 8) upon those who are in Christ, and it is not done in an ill-conceived manner or haphazardly but "in all wisdom and insight" (v. 8). Just as God purposefully chooses, predestines, adopts, and redeems sinners, so too he chooses to lavish his kindness and favor upon them in accordance with his infinite wisdom and insight.

God redeems us according to his divine plan: In the past, the plan of God to redeem a people through his Son was shrouded in mystery. Although it was God's design all along to send a Messiah to crush the head of the serpent, some of the details of his plan were not disclosed. In the gospel, however, God has revealed what Paul calls his "mystery," which involves uniting all things in Christ (v. 9). In particular, it relates to God's plan to unite all things (including Jews and gentiles) into the one body of Christ (see Rom 11:25; 16:25–27; Eph 3:3, 4, 9; Col 1:26–27;

1 Tim 3:16). God set forth this plan in "the fullness of time" (see Gal 4:4), a plan "to unite all things" through his Son (Eph 1:10).

REFLECT ON CHRIST

Notice once again the centrality of Christ in the plan of God: our redemption is possible because we are "in him," and it is secured through his blood (1:7). Our redemption comes to us freely, but it comes at the great price of Christ's death on the cross. Our salvation has been paid for by another, and the cost was immense. Jesus paid it all.

Furthermore, God's plan was set forth "in Christ" (1:9), a plan to unite all things "in him" (1:10). Christ was intimately involved in planning redemption with the Father. He is not only the means by which God will unite all the disparate elements of creation together; he is the center and focal point through whom, and for whom, all this will take place.

In Colossians, Paul offers another powerful reminder of the centrality of Jesus in God's plan: "For by him all things were created, in heaven and on earth, visible and invisible, whether thrones or dominions or rulers or authorities—all things were created through him and for him ... to reconcile to himself all things, whether on earth or in heaven, making peace by the blood of his cross" (Col 1:16, 20).

APPLY GOD'S WORD

Paul's exhortation to his readers is that God should be blessed (praised) because of how much he has blessed us. In verses 7–10, the focus is on God's work of redemption and the forgiveness of our sins. Do you view yourself as having been redeemed? Note that this redemption is not simply a future hope but a present reality: "we have redemption" (1:7).

Although the full impact of our redemption is still to come (the resurrection of our bodies and dwelling in God's presence), we have been given a foretaste as our sins are forgiven and God's Spirit dwells in us (1:13).

Do you view your sins as being forgiven? Not just some of them but all of them? Not just the small ones but the big ones too? Not just those in the past but those that will occur in the future? It is when we contemplate our current standing before God as those redeemed and forgiven that we begin to truly praise God. Jesus said, regarding the woman (a "sinner") who anointed him, "Therefore I tell you, her sins, which are many, are forgiven—for she loved much. But he who is forgiven little, loves little" (Luke 7:47). When we contemplate the depths of our sin and the height of his lavish grace, we will praise God.

PRAY

God, I thank you that you have redeemed me and removed my sin as far as the east is from the west. You are worthy to be praised because of the rich grace that you have lavished on me because of your Son. He paid it all, and so all to him I owe. Amen.

STUDY IT FURTHER

1. Paul speaks often of the "blood" of Jesus. Read Romans 3:25; 5:9; Ephesians 2:13; and Colossians 1:20, and describe the benefits believers receive because of Jesus's sacrifice (i.e., his blood).

2. Read Luke 7:36–47, and list several principles that this passage teaches us about forgiveness.

3. Paul uses several words that reveal God's future intent for his creation: "will" (1:9), "purpose" (1:9), and "plan" (1:10). God's will/purpose/plan are according to his wisdom and insight, which are perfect. How does that give you confidence in him and his plan, even when the path ahead seems difficult?

Day 4

Ephesians 1:11–12

READ

In him we have obtained an inheritance, having been predestined according to the purpose of him who works all things according to the counsel of his will, so that we who were the first to hope in Christ might be to the praise of his glory.

MEDITATE

Paul now provides us with a third reason that God is worthy to be praised: he has given us an *inheritance*. The repetition of the phrase "in him" (in Jesus) demonstrates that verse 11 is parallel to verses 7 and 13. Although the verb translated "we have obtained an inheritance" occurs only here in the New Testament, the theme of believers receiving an inheritance is also mentioned in verses 5 ("adoption"), 14 ("inheritance"), and 18 ("glorious inheritance").

God provides for us a present inheritance: This inheritance is not just future; it is present. Paul says, "We *have* obtained an inheritance" (1:11). An inheritance is usually received upon the death of a relative or friend. It is something we do not have access to until the passing of someone close to us, even though it might be promised to us. Through Christ's death, Paul states we have an inheritance now. It is ours. And yet, it is not fully ours. We have the promise of an inheritance that can only be fully realized when we enter eternity.

God provides for us a certain inheritance: Paul states that believers have an inheritance since they have "been predestined according to [God's] purpose" (1:11). Believers are guaranteed to receive their inheritance because God has predestined them to possess it. Just as believers were predestined for adoption "according to the purpose of his will" (1:5), so too we are predestined to receive an inheritance "according to the purpose of him who works all things according to the counsel of his will" (1:11). This is good news. God was delighted to choose a people for himself even while we were his enemies (Rom 5:8–10). His intention is firm and secure. Paul uses the words "purpose," "counsel," and "will" to describe God's choice. This plan was carefully considered and carried out by the sovereign creator of the universe. So Paul encourages us to consider our privileged position as those chosen by God and those who have a certain inheritance.

God provides for us an imperishable inheritance: Because this inheritance is obtained "in him" (Christ), it is not merely a passing, perishable inheritance. It is secured by the eternal Lord who guarantees and grants "every spiritual blessing" to all who are found in him (1:3). The apostle Peter similarly writes, "According to his great mercy, he has caused us to be born again to a living hope through the resurrection of Jesus Christ from the dead, to an inheritance that is imperishable, undefiled, and unfading, kept in heaven for you" (1 Pet 1:3–4).

God provides for us a glorious inheritance: Finally, the inheritance ultimately points to God's glory. Paul indicates that believers are predestined to receive an inheritance so that they might praise God's glory (1:12). God's glory is the revelation and manifestation of who he is, including his essence, power, majesty, purity, and holiness. To praise God for his glory is to declare (publicly and privately) that he is the one true God who made heaven and earth, and he is, therefore, the sovereign Lord in control of all things. The glorious God has promised us a glorious inheritance.

REFLECT ON CHRIST

Our present and future inheritance is bound up with our relationship with Christ. God chose us and predestined us to an inheritance, and the Spirit seals us to guarantee our inheritance, but it is Christ who purchases and secures our inheritance. Christ lived a perfect life, obeying all of God's laws so that there was no fault in him. He died a perfect death, paying the debt of the undeserving so that their sins were erased. He conquered the grave and rose from the dead on the third day. And he sits at God's right hand, reigning over his creation.

It is only those who are in Christ who have access to this inheritance. Only when we have a personal relationship with God through Christ are we incorporated into the family of God. Through our acceptance of God's Son, we become the true children of Abraham and thus heirs to the promises given to Abraham, which were ultimately fulfilled in Christ. Paul further describes himself and others as those "who hope in Christ" (1:12). It is only those who believe and hope in Christ who will receive this glorious inheritance.

APPLY GOD'S WORD

We have yet another reason to praise God: He has blessed us with a certain and imperishable inheritance. This inheritance is free to all who trust and hope in Christ. It would be a tragedy, however, to know about this glorious inheritance and not receive it. Although it is open to all freely, it is available only to those who will place their faith in Christ. Now is the day of salvation! Be sure that you have turned from your sin and have trusted in Jesus to save you. Once we declare Christ as our savior, we become part of God's family and coheirs with Christ.

Further, this passage should cause us to reflect on God's gracious plan to redeem a people for himself. He predestined us according to his purpose. He works all things according to the counsel of his will and for the good of those who love him and who are called according to his purpose (see Rom 8:28). He allowed us to hear the gospel of Jesus Christ. He granted us repentance and faith to receive that message. He provides us an eternal inheritance of being in his presence forever. All of this should cause us to offer our lives "to the praise of his glory" (Eph 1:12).

PRAY

Thank you, God, for the hope that I have awaiting me—
eternity with you where there are no more tears, no more
pain, no more suffering, and no more sin. I long for the day
when my faith will be made sight. Until then,
strengthen my faith by reminding me
of the glorious inheritance that awaits me.
And may this hope cause me to praise your name. Amen.

STUDY IT FURTHER

1. Read Romans 8:16–17; Galatians 3:29, and 4:4–7. What do these passages teach us about being an heir of God?

2. In the Old Testament, the people of God expected to inherit the promised land. How do Jesus and the New Testament authors portray the object of our inheritance (see Matt 5:10; Eph 5:5; Jas 2:5)?

3. Apart from Christ and his transforming Spirit, we have no legitimate claim to an inheritance (1 Cor 6:9; 15:50; Gal 5:21). How can you demonstrate your gratitude to God for his promise of a glorious inheritance today?

Day 5

Ephesians 1:13–14

READ

In him you also, when you heard the word of truth, the gospel of your salvation, and believed in him, were sealed with the promised Holy Spirit, who is the guarantee of our inheritance until we acquire possession of it, to the praise of his glory.

MEDITATE

With the repetition of the phrase "in him," Paul signals the fourth reason that God is worthy to be praised: he has sealed us with the Holy Spirit. This final reason provides an important link to the previous reasons that Paul has offered: God chooses us, redeems us, and gives us an inheritance. But what if we fall and never receive what God has promised us in Christ? What if we don't have the strength or belief to persevere until the end? Here is where Paul offers us hope: God seals us with his Spirit, who will guarantee our inheritance. That is, the Spirit not only indwells his people; he is the means by which we are sealed so as to guarantee that we receive our promised inheritance.

God seals us with the promised Spirit: The Spirit of God is described as "promised." In the Old Testament, the Spirit was promised to the people of Israel. Isaiah states, "I will pour out my Spirit on your offspring, and my blessing on your descendants" (Isa 44:3). Ezekiel adds, "And I will give them one heart, and a new spirit I will put within them. I will remove the heart of stone from their flesh and give them a heart of flesh, that they may walk in my statutes and keep my rules and obey them" (Ezek 11:19–20). As the new-covenant people of God, we are given a new heart, and God's Spirit indwells us.

God seals us so that we may have a secure inheritance: Not only are we *given* the Spirit, but we are *sealed* with the Spirit. We are protected from God's future wrath and judgment that will be poured out on the world. When Paul references that the good news of Jesus is "the gospel of [our] *salvation*" (1:13, emphasis added), the implication is that believers are saved from some sort of danger. Indeed, the danger we are rescued from is the wrath of God that will be revealed against all ungodliness (Rom 1:18). The Spirit serves as a deposit or down payment that guarantees we will inherit our future inheritance. More specifically, the Spirit serves as an assurance that we will receive all that Christ has accomplished for us. When we hear the gospel message and truly believe it, we are *sealed* with the Holy Spirit. God therefore claims us as his own and secures our future inheritance.

The term "guarantee" in Greek (*arrabōn*) is found only three times in the New Testament, always in reference to the Holy Spirit (see 2 Cor 1:22; 5:5). In the ancient world, a guarantee served as a down payment for something with the expectation that the full amount would be given once the terms of the agreement were fulfilled. It was a small portion (foretaste) of more that was to follow. In other words, God has given us his Spirit "until we acquire possession of [our inheritance]" (1:14). This inheritance will include the blessing of unending fellowship with God. As both the psalmist and Jeremiah proclaim, "The LORD is my portion" (Ps 16:5; 119:57; Lam 3:24). Praise God for his plan to choose us, redeem us, grant us an inheritance, and seal us with the promised Holy Spirit.

REFLECT ON CHRIST

This passage again reminds us of the amazing work of the Triune God. The Father chooses us and provides us an inheritance, the Son redeems us, and the Spirit seals us. The Trinity is on full display in this passage. And yet, even when Paul is reminding us of the work of the Spirit, the work of the Son is emphasized since they are intimately connected. We are sealed with the promised Holy Spirit "in him" (in Christ). It is only when we are united to Christ that we receive the Spirit of Christ. Additionally, the Spirit seals only those who hear the gospel message and believe in Christ. Faith in Christ (his work, death, resurrection, and ascension) is necessary to receive the Spirit.

Finally, that fact that the Spirit is the guarantee of our inheritance reminds us that our inheritance was not given to us because we earned or deserved it. Indeed, we owed a debt we could not pay, but through the work of Christ, we now receive abundant blessings. We are given that which was secured by another. We only receive what Christ has earned because we are in him.

APPLY GOD'S WORD

This passage is full of hope and encouragement for those who have "heard the word of truth, the gospel" and have "believed in him." Do you live with the hope of a future inheritance? Those who trust in Christ and have received his Spirit will receive an incredible inheritance. Knowing that we will receive such blessings should affect the way we think and live today. How have you been transformed by the hope of an eternal inheritance? What about your life has changed because you know that this life is not the end? Let us consider the powerful force of Christ in our lives now and praise God for the hope of a secure inheritance in our future.

The result of God's favor on us (which includes being sealed with the Holy Spirit) should lead us to praise and exalt his name ("to the praise of his glory"). Not only does Paul begin this passage with a call to praise God, but he ends by praising God for his amazing blessings.

PRAY

Dear Triune God—Father, Son, Holy Spirit—thank you for the great salvation that you have provided for me. Not only have you rescued me from sin and death,
but you have sealed me with your Spirit,
securing my future inheritance.
Praise be to your glorious name! Amen.

STUDY IT FURTHER

1. Read Ezekiel 36:26–27 and 37:14. What do these passages teach us about the coming of the Spirit in the lives of God's people?

2. Read 2 Corinthians 1:22 and 5:5 (see also Rom 8:23). What do each of these texts add to our understanding of the Spirit serving as a guarantee of our inheritance?

3. In Ephesians 4:30, Paul indicates that God's people are not to grieve the Holy Spirit "by whom you were sealed for the day of redemption." Why do you suppose that Paul once again emphasizes our being sealed with the Spirit?

Day 6

Ephesians 1:15–17

READ

For this reason, because I have heard of your faith in the Lord Jesus and your love toward all the saints, I do not cease to give thanks for you, remembering you in my prayers, that the God of our Lord Jesus Christ, the Father of glory, may give you the Spirit of wisdom and of revelation in the knowledge of him ...

MEDITATE

Thanksgiving and prayer should mark a Christian. There will always be issues that pull our thoughts downward into doom, doubt, and distraction. This passage, however, reminds us of the importance of giving thanks to God for others and praying for them. After praising God for his blessings of election, redemption, adoption, and preservation, Paul offers thanks for the faith and love of the Ephesian believers. Whenever Paul prayed to God on behalf of others, he was in the habit of giving thanks for their belief in the Lord Jesus Christ and their unselfish love for other believers. Paul didn't only pray this way for the Ephesian church. He also prayed for other churches. For example, he prays for the church in Colossae: "We always thank God, the Father of our Lord Jesus Christ, when we pray for you, since we heard of your faith in Christ Jesus and of the love that you have for all the saints" (Col 1:3–4).

Ephesus was certainly not an easy place to be a Christian. Believers there lived in a hostile environment because Christianity was marginalized, and Christians often suffered persecution. In Acts 19, Demetrius the silversmith incited a riot against Paul, and the mob cried out, "Great is Artemis of the Ephesians," for two hours (see Acts 19:21–41). It was in this city that the followers of Jesus to whom Paul writes held firmly to their faith. In addition to their faith, Paul gives thanks for their love "toward all the saints" (1:15). "Saints" refers to all believers who have been sanctified (set apart or made holy) by the redemption secured by Christ (see 1:1, 18). Thus, Paul celebrated both the faith and the love of the believers in Ephesus.

We should pray regularly: Beginning in 1:16, Paul transitions from thanksgiving to intercessory prayer. Paul often prayed for the recipients of his letters (see Rom 1:9; Phil 1:3–4; 1 Thess 1:2; 2 Tim 1:3; Phlm 4). He reveals that he did not cease to pray for the Ephesian believers, as he remembered them in his prayers (1:16). Elsewhere, he exhorts believers to "pray without ceasing" (1 Thess 5:17). Christians should regularly pray for each other.

We should pray thankfully: When Paul prayed for the Ephesians, he gave thanks to God for them. Certainly, Paul would have experienced disappointment and frustration with them. Yet, in his prayers, he was able to thank God for the good things that God was doing among them. Christians should be thankful for the work of God in others.

We should pray meaningfully: Interestingly, these prayers are not for worldly blessings (health and wealth) but for the spiritual well-being of his readers. Paul asks "the God of our

Lord Jesus Christ" to give the Ephesian believers "the Spirit of wisdom and revelation" (1:17). The Spirit illuminates our hearts and minds so that the knowledge of God as revealed through his word is embraced and cherished. Consequently, although we are already sealed with God's Spirit (1:13), we still need to be filled and walk according to the Spirit. Paul often prays that his readers will increase in their knowledge of God. Paul prays for the Philippians that their "love may abound more and more, with knowledge and all discernment" (Phil 1:9). He prays for the Colossians that they "may be filled with all knowledge of his will in all spiritual wisdom and understanding" (Col 1:9–10). And he prays that Philemon's witness in sharing his faith "may become effective for the full knowledge of every good thing that is in us for the sake of Christ" (Phlm 6). May we pray regularly, thankfully, and meaningfully.

REFLECT ON CHRIST

The centrality of Christ in the life of the believer is clearly seen in this passage. First, Jesus is given the title "Lord" (1:15, 17). He is "Lord" because he is the one who conquered sin, death, and the devil and reigns on his throne at God's right hand. He is the Lord of heaven and earth, and he reigns as king above all other powers. All enemies will be crushed under his feet. Second, he is the object of faith. Paul states that one's faith is "in the Lord Jesus" (1:15). Having faith is not sufficient. Millions of people place their faith in something that cannot save them. But our faith is *in Jesus*, the reigning Lord. He alone *can* save, and he alone *will* save those who trust in him. When we place our faith in Jesus, he grants us his Spirit to dwell in us, giving us wisdom and illuminating God's revelation. Third, Jesus is referenced as Lord in relation to God the Father, who is called "the God of our Lord Jesus Christ" (1:17). God the Father and

Jesus the Son are intimately connected. So much so that God is referenced in relation to Jesus. Indeed, the Son has accomplished all that the Father purposed for him to do.

APPLY GOD'S WORD

Twice in Ephesians Paul earnestly prays for the Ephesian believers (1:16–23; 3:14–21). He didn't just instruct them but modeled Christlike behavior to them. He regularly prayed for them. True love for others expresses itself in heartfelt prayers. What can you do to get in the habit of praying regularly for others?

Do you pray that others will be drawn closer to God through his Spirit? Paul's prayers aren't fixated on asking for earthly comforts or the healing of bodily ailments. Instead, he prays that his readers will know God more. Praying for God's healing is not wrong, but praying for a deeper understanding of God and his word is even better. Use Paul's prayers as a model for how to pray for others.

In Ephesians 6:12, Paul states that our battle is not against people (flesh and blood) but against spiritual forces. Knowing this, he exhorts his readers to pray "at all times in the Spirit" (6:18). He also asks the Ephesian believers to pray for him (6:19–20). Are you ready and willing to pray for the spiritual needs of others as well as share your needs with them?

PRAY

O God of our Lord Jesus Christ, the Father of glory,
we give thanks for all the people we know who confess Jesus
as Lord. Help us to pray for them regularly. God, through
your Spirit, fill them with wisdom and understanding
so that they might know you more.
Open their eyes and open our eyes so that we
might all see and behold your glory. Amen.

STUDY IT FURTHER

1. Read Paul's prayers in Philippians 1:9–11; 1 Thessalonians 3:9–13; and 2 Thessalonians 1:11–12. What common themes emerge in these prayers? How might Paul's prayers be an example of how we should pray?

2. What does it mean that God is "the Father of glory" (1:17)? Read Psalm 24:7–10; 29:3–4; Acts 7:2; 1 Corinthians 2:8; and James 2:1 to see other contexts where God's glory is mentioned.

3. Do you think Isaiah 11:2 ("And the Spirit of the LORD shall rest upon him, the Spirit of wisdom and understanding, the Spirit of counsel and might, the Spirit of knowledge and the fear of the LORD") provides background for Paul's comments in verse 17? Why or why not?

Day 7

Ephesians 1:18–23

READ

… having the eyes of your hearts enlightened, that you may
know what is the hope to which he has called you,
what are the riches of his glorious inheritance in the saints,
and what is the immeasurable greatness of his power
toward us who believe, according to the working of his great
might that he worked in Christ when he raised him
from the dead and seated him at his right hand in the
heavenly places, far above all rule and authority and power
and dominion, and above every name
that is named, not only in this age but also
in the one to come. And he put all things under his feet and
gave him as head over all things to the church,
which is his body, the fullness of him who fills all in all.

MEDITATE

In the previous verse, Paul opened his prayer by asking God to give believers "the Spirit of wisdom and of revelation" (1:17). In 1:18–23, he continues his intercessory prayer by requesting that God would grant us spiritual insight so that we will comprehend three important truths: (1) the hope to which God has called us, (2) the riches of our glorious inheritance, and (3) the immeasurable greatness of God's power, especially as it is displayed in Christ.

We should pray that others will know the hope of God's calling: Not only has God graciously predestined or chosen us to be his people and called us through the preaching of the gospel, he has also filled us with hope. Before embracing God's Son—the only remedy for sin—we had "no hope" and were "without God in the world" (2:12). But now, through Christ's atoning work on the cross, we who were once without hope have been called to a sure hope. We should pray for this hope to be seen by others.

We should pray that others will know the riches of God's glorious inheritance: In 1:14, Paul declares that when we hear and believe the gospel, we are sealed with the Holy Spirit "who is the guarantee of our inheritance." Similarly, in Colossians 1:12 he prays that we would thank God who qualifies us "to share in the inheritance of the saints." This inheritance is described with the words "riches" and "glorious." As Paul later states, God "is able to do far more than we ask or think" (Eph 3:20). We should pray that God's glorious inheritance will be experienced by others.

We should pray that others will know the immeasurable greatness of God's power: This is the same power that raised Jesus from the dead, seated him at God's side, and gave him authority over all things. Paul stresses God's power by describing it as a power of "immeasurable greatness," which is "according to the working of his great might." Ephesus was steeped in magic practices and the cult of Artemis. Paul reassures the Ephesian Christians with the supremacy of God's power over all creation.

This power is preeminently displayed in Christ. We should pray that God's power will be known by others.

In 1:20–23, Paul expands on the power of God in relation to Christ, specifically his resurrection, exaltation, subjugation, and his domination. First, the power of God raised Jesus from the dead. The resurrection of Jesus is the climax of God's work in history; sin, death, and the devil were defeated by Jesus's work on the cross, which was validated by the resurrection. Second, God's power exalted Christ by seating him at the Father's right hand in heaven (1:20–21). This position signifies Jesus's lordship (he is seated on a throne), honor and power (he is seated at God's right hand), and prominence (he is seated in the heavenly places). Third, the power of God has subjected all things under Christ's feet (1:22). This description echoes Psalm 8:6: "You have put all things under his feet." Although Christ is currently ruling and will claim the final victory, the final subjugation is not yet complete until death is defeated and the devil is judged. Finally, God's power made Christ head over the church—domination (1:22–23). Not only has God made Christ ruler over "all things" (including the hostile principalities and powers), but Paul explicitly notes that his headship (ruling authority) extends to the church. So, Paul's prayer is that God's people will comprehend the amazing power of God that he works for our advantage.

REFLECT ON CHRIST

As Paul prays for his readers, he prays that God would give them a Spirit of wisdom and revelation and that they might comprehend the immensity of God grace—a grace that is revealed through God's calling, inheritance, and power. But Paul's prayer flows seamlessly from his requests regarding his readers to the glories of Christ. Specifically, his last request is that we would comprehend God's great power, a power that is most clearly displayed in Christ. Interestingly, about half the verses in this section (1:15–23) focus on the power of God as revealed in Christ (1:19–23). The power of God is best illustrated by the person and work of Christ. It is the power of God that raised Christ from the dead. It is the power of God that enables Christ to reign in heaven at his right hand. It is the power of God that subjects all things to Christ's lordship. It is the power of God that placed Christ as the head over the church. When we think of God's power, we should think of Christ's life, death, resurrection, ascension, and reign. Prayers of thanksgiving are rooted and grounded in God's power revealed in Christ.

APPLY GOD'S WORD

Paul's first prayer for the Ephesian believers is a model for us. He prayed for them because he was concerned for them and because he loved them. He prayed that they would comprehend the hope of their calling, the riches of their inheritance, and the power of God that is displayed in Christ but is now directed toward the believer. Likewise, if we desire our friends and family to submit to God and his will, we should pray for them. In his other letters, Paul urges his readers to be steadfast in prayer (Rom 12:12; Eph 6:18; Phil 4:6; Col 4:2; 1 Thess 5:17; 1 Tim 2:1, 8).

Based on Paul's example of prayer and his apostolic exhortations to pray, we can see that prayer is essential in the life of the believer. How essential has prayer been in your life the past week? What step could you take to make prayer more central?

Paul's prayer highlights three areas in which he desires us to grow—our knowledge of our sure hope, our rich inheritance, and our powerful God. All of these truths are revealed in God's word. In essence, Paul is praying that we would read, recall, and reflect on God's word. Is it your normal practice to meditate on Scripture throughout the day? Consider developing a rhythm that helps you recall throughout the day truth related to your Bible reading.

PRAY

Dear God, please open my spiritual eyes that I might know
the truth of your word in a deeper way—
that I would know the hope to which you have called me;
that I would know the riches of your glorious inheritance;
that I would know the immeasurable greatness
of your power. Thank you that your power
is most clearly seen in your Son, Jesus Christ. Amen.

STUDY IT FURTHER

1. Read Paul's exhortations for believers to pray in Romans 12:12; Ephesians 6:18; Philippians 4:6; Colossians 4:2; and 1 Thessalonians 5:17. What do these passages teach us about *when* believers should pray and *what* we should pray?

2. The resurrection represents the pinnacle of God's work in salvation history, which is seen in the preaching of the apostles (e.g., Acts 2:23–24; 17:18; 1 Cor 15:3–4). How would you defend the physical resurrection of Christ to someone who is skeptical?

3. Paul reminds us that Jesus is now seated at God's right hand. This metaphor conveys both honor and power. Read Exodus 15:6; Psalm 89:13; Isaiah 48:13; Romans 8:34; Colossians 3:1; Hebrews 1:3; 8:1; 10:12; 12:2; and 1 Peter 3:22. What do these passages teach us about Christ's *honor* and his *power*?

Day 8

Ephesians 2:1–3

READ

And you were dead in the trespasses and sins
in which you once walked, following the course
of this world, following the prince of the power of the air,
the spirit that is now at work in the sons of disobedience—
among whom we all once lived in the passions of our flesh,
carrying out the desires of the body and the mind,
and were by nature children of wrath,
like the rest of mankind.

MEDITATE

In one sense, our culture tends to avoid the reality of death—we don't like to think about our mortality. But in another sense, our culture has a fascination with the dead (think of all the zombie shows and true crime podcasts). In this passage, Paul presents the natural state of humanity as those who are spiritually dead. Not spiritually sick or weak and in need of medicine, but those who are spiritually dead and in need of new life. Consequently, everyone not with God is under God's wrath.

Paul describes the pre-conversion state of believers as those who were "dead in the trespasses and sins" (2:1). This description applies to all of humanity, not just the most depraved of society. Prior to our conversion, we lived in rebellion to God by breaking his commands and sinning against him. Our predicament before our conversion was dire. Paul notes three influences that led us toward the path of destruction: the world, the devil, and the flesh.

Before our conversion, we followed the world: First, Paul states that we formerly followed "the course of this world" (2:2). In this context, the term "world" refers to that which is opposed to God—that is, the cultural, social, political, or economic ideologies or forces that are hostile to God and his ways. Before knowing Christ, our preferences, attitudes, and habits were often contrary to God's standard and were according to the standards of this world. The apostle John warned his readers, "Do not love the world or the things in the world. If anyone loves the world, the love of the Father is not in him" (1 John 2:15).

Before our conversion, we followed the devil: Second, Paul reminds us that we formerly followed "the prince of the power of the air" (2:2), a clear reference to the devil or Satan. The Bible presents evil forces as alive and active in the world today. Satan is ready to take advantage of believers when they sin (4:27). Christians therefore need to clothe themselves with God's armor to stand against the attacks of the devil (6:11, 16). In the Gospels, the devil is called the "prince [or ruler] of demons" (Matt 9:34) and "the ruler of this world" (John 12:31). In 2 Corinthians 4:4, he is called "the god of this world" who blinds unbelievers from seeing the truth. He sets traps or snares for the unwary (1 Tim 3:7; 2 Tim 2:26) and prowls around like a lion seeking to devour his foes (1 Pet 5:8). John states that "the whole world lies in the power of the evil one" (1 John 5:19). The devil is a spiritual being working to destroy humanity.

Before our conversion, we followed our flesh: Third, we are corrupted by our own flesh. By "flesh" Paul is not referring to the physical body or our physical existence but to our fallen, self-centered human nature. We are not only influenced by external forces; our own hearts lead us astray, causing us to sin against God and against others. Consequently, we were designated as "children of wrath" (2:3). The natural condition of fallen humanity is grim and bleak. Thankfully the passage doesn't stop here.

REFLECT ON CHRIST

Today's passage does not include the good news of Jesus Christ but tells the bad news of our condition apart from Christ. Apart from Christ we are dead in our sins. Apart from Christ we follow the prince of the power of the air—the devil. Apart from Christ we live according to the passions of the flesh—our sinful nature. Apart from Christ we are children of wrath. The message is clear. A Christ-less existence is one of rebellion against God, and it ends in destruction.

Humanity is not merely sick or ailing but spiritually bankrupt. A dead person cannot change their situation. They need miraculous intervention to bring them back to life. We cannot improve our standing before God because, apart from Christ, we have neither the ability nor the desire to do so. Only new life through our union with Christ can change our predicament.

APPLY GOD'S WORD

It is perhaps difficult to view ourselves as formerly dead spiritually when we were alive physically. Earlier in Ephesians, Paul prayed that God would open or enlighten the eyes of our hearts. It takes prayer and faith to believe spiritual realities as we stand in a physical world. Paul reminds us that we were dead in our sins, deceived by the devil, dominated by our sinful nature, and doomed to receive God's wrath. But God has another plan for those who come to him in faith.

God is holy and must punish sin. For him to ignore or dismiss our sin is contrary to his nature and would be a violation of his own standard. Thankfully, God is also loving. Because God is both holy and loving, he led Jesus to the cross. The wrath of God is absorbed by Jesus, and new life is given to all who look to Christ in faith, placing their allegiance in him. Thanks be to God that we are not left in our sins. Thanks be to God that we are not left following the ways of the devil and the desires of our corrupt hearts. Thanks be to God that we are not under God's wrath but are now counted as beloved.

PRAY

O God, I recognize that apart from you I can do nothing.
I recognize that apart from you I gladly followed
the world, the devil, and the flesh and was justly under
your wrath. But I also recognize that you did not leave
me there because of your great grace. Thank you. Amen.

STUDY IT FURTHER

1. Prior to our conversion, this passage describes us as "dead" (2:1) and as "children of wrath" (2:3). How does Paul describe us in Romans 5:6–10? What caused our spiritual death (see Rom 5:12)?

2. The devil is described as "the prince of the power of the air" (2:2) who is active in the world today. At the same time,

it is important for Christians to remember that Satan is a defeated foe. Read Ephesians 1:21; Colossians 2:15; Hebrews 2:14; and 1 John 3:8. How is Satan's influence limited and his doom certain?

3. What does Paul mean when he states that we were "by nature" children of wrath (see Gal 2:15)?

Day 9

Ephesians 2:4

READ

But God, being rich in mercy,
because of the great love with which he loved us ...

MEDITATE

The famous Welsh preacher Dr. Martyn Lloyd-Jones (1899–1981), who ministered for almost thirty years at Westminster Chapel in London, preached a sermon that later became known as his "But God" sermon. The focus of the message was Paul's Spirit-inspired words from Ephesians 2:4. He focused on the words "but God" because they change the doomed picture of humanity Paul has been painting. Instead of a bleak demise, these words introduce surprise, hope, the supernatural work of God, and salvation. Let's look at how the bad news highlights the grace of God's good news.

The bad news: No one likes to hear bad news. We often experience that sinking feeling in our stomach when someone tells us that they have bad news to share with us. In Ephesians 2:1–3, Paul details the spiritual situation of fallen humanity apart from God's intervening grace. The prognosis is not that humanity is sick or in critical condition. Rather, the stark reality is that we are spiritually dead. Because we are dead in our sins, we are influenced by the world, the devil, and the flesh. That is, we live according to our nature. Because our nature is fallen, so are our desires, marking us as children of "disobedience" (2:2) and "wrath" (2:3). All of those without a relationship with Christ are deserving of God's wrath and await final judgment. Thankfully, this is not the end of the story.

The good news: Paul has given us the bad news so that we can comprehend the glory of God in the good news he shares next. Paul's main point is to highlight the grace of God, who saves those who are dead and undeserving. Notice that Paul's remedy for our dire predicament does not begin with our obedience to God and his commands. Obedience is not possible for those who are spiritually dead. Instead, the remedy begins with God: "But God ..." New life is needed before true obedience can be attained. Trying harder to appease God and earn his favor is never the right solution. Rather, when we recognize our true dilemma, the incredible mercy and love of God, and the subsequent new life that we were gifted, then true obedience will occur in our lives.

Paul reminds us that our salvation is based on God's mercy and love. These characteristics of God can be found throughout the Bible. For example, Exodus 34:6 states, "The LORD, the LORD, a God merciful and gracious, slow to anger, and abounding in steadfast love and faithfulness." Psalm 103:8 proclaims, "The LORD is merciful and gracious, slow to anger and abounding in steadfast love." Similarly, in the New Testament we read, "He saved us, not because of works done by us in righteousness, but according to his own mercy" (Titus 3:5). God is *rich* in mercy and loves us with his *great* love. Mercy and love are what stand behind God's decision to call us out of darkness and into his marvelous light. We were dead in our trespasses and sins ... but God!

REFLECT ON CHRIST

Up to this point, our passage (Eph 2:1–4) does not mention Christ. We were dead in our sins and destined for wrath, but God had mercy on us because of his love. But God's rich mercy and great love do not exist in the abstract. They don't reach us *directly,* as if God can simply ignore our disloyalty and sin and pretend they never occurred. God's mercy and love always flow to us *through Christ.* In other words, how is it that God brings us to life from our state of death? It is through Christ's life, death, and resurrection. How is it that God cancels our debt and receives us as his children? It is through Christ's life, death, and resurrection. How is it that God gives us new affections so that we no longer are slaves to the world, the devil, and the flesh? It is through Christ's life, death, and resurrection. How is it that God raises us and seats us in the heavenly places? It is through Christ's life, death, and resurrection. Praise God for his mercy and love shown to us through his Son, Jesus Christ.

APPLY GOD'S WORD

Paul begins Ephesians by praising God since he has blessed us with every spiritual blessing in the heavenly places (1:3–14). This should also be our response when we come to realize (or are reminded) that he took the initiative to reestablish a relationship with us. He predestined us, redeemed us, adopted us, and sealed us with the Spirit (1:3–14). He is the one who regenerates us (gives us new life) and gives us new affections so that we no longer seek to fulfill the desires of the flesh.

When things are difficult today, remember that you were destined for wrath ... but God. When you don't feel loved or appreciated today, remember God's rich mercy and great love for you. These truths should cause us to stop and be thankful to God. As the psalmist says, "Oh give thanks to the LORD, for he is good; for his steadfast love endures forever!" (Ps 118:1).

PRAY

Oh God, what words could express to you my profound
sense of gratitude for your mercy and love
that you showered on me through your Son,
Jesus Christ? Receive my thanksgiving as a sweet-smelling
aroma. I was lost but now I'm found!
I was blind but now I see! And I was dead, but now
I am alive! Thanks be to your holy name. Amen.

STUDY IT FURTHER

1. Read Jonah 4:1–2. Because Jonah knew that God was gracious and merciful, he didn't want to bring the message of judgment to Nineveh, lest the people of Nineveh hear the warning and repent. Are there times that we attempt to restrict the message of God's mercy?

2. Read Romans 5:5–8 and 8:39. What do these passages teach us about God's love?

3. Read Psalm 118, and list all the reasons it gives for why we should give thanks to the Lord.

Day 10

Ephesians 2:5–7

READ

... even when we were dead in our trespasses,
made us alive together with Christ—by grace you have been
saved—and raised us up with him and seated us with him in
the heavenly places in Christ Jesus, so that
in the coming ages he might show the immeasurable
riches of his grace in kindness toward us in Christ Jesus.

MEDITATE

After detailing the bad news of our fallen condition, Paul expands on the good news that was introduced by the phrase "But God" in verse 4. In order to make the contrast crystal clear, Paul repeats the reality that God saved us "when we were dead in our trespasses" (v. 5). Paul then uses three verbs to describe God's gracious work in saving sinners—all of which emphasize a believer's union with Christ. A simplified version of the sentence reads: "God ... *made us alive* together with Christ ... and *raised us up* with him and *seated us* with him" (emphases added, 2:4–6). All that God does for us, he does for us because of our relationship with Christ. And all that God does for us, he first accomplished in Christ.

In Christ, God makes us alive: We were dead in our trespasses and sins. We were living in rebellion to God and his law. We were unable and unwilling to submit to him and his lordship over us. But God made us alive. He breathed new life into us through the regenerating work of the Spirit. Just as Jesus lay dead in the tomb for three days until he was brought to life through the power of God, so we are brought to life through that same resurrection power. After noting God's life-giving power, Paul pauses to remind us of the reason for this transformation from death to life. He adds, "By grace you have been saved" (v. 5). It is only because of God's grace that we receive new life.

In Christ, God raises us up: Because we are made alive by God's power, we are then raised to participate in this new life. Of course, unlike Christ's resurrection (which was physical), Paul is speaking metaphorically of our spiritual resurrection. But this spiritual resurrection is based on Christ's physical resurrection and will ultimately result in our physical resurrection.

In Christ, God seats us in the heavenly places: Again, this concept is used metaphorically since we are not physically seated in heaven. But just as Christ was exalted and now reigns over his creation, so too we share in his reign, even now. Throughout this passage, Paul parallels the work that God *did* in Christ and the work he *does* in us. All the blessings we have, we have because of our union with Christ.

All of God's work in us (new life and new status) is part of God's grand purpose. It is done so that "he might show the immeasurable riches of his grace" (2:7). Earlier, Paul emphasized that the ultimate goal of salvation is the glory of God (1:6, 12, 14). Here, Paul reminds us that God saves rebellious sinners to display God's grace—a grace that is immeasurably rich and full of kindness. Furthermore, this display of grace is not only for this age but for the coming ages. The "coming ages" most likely refers to the unending epochs of time that will encompass all of eternity. God's glory will be on display forever.

REFLECT ON CHRIST

Paul highlights the believer's union with Christ in at least six ways in this passage. Three times he adds the phrase "in/with Christ Jesus": (1) we are made alive together *with Christ*; (2) we are raised and seated in heaven *in Christ Jesus*; and (3) we are shown grace and kindness *in Christ Jesus*. Additionally, Paul uses three verbs that contain the prepositional prefix meaning "together with": (1) we are *made alive together with* Christ; (2) we are *raised together with* Christ; and (3) we are *seated together with* Christ.

The Christian faith is not a merit-based religion. It is a grace-based religion: "by grace you have been saved" (v. 5). All that we have is not because *we* earned it but because *Christ* earned it for us. We are the recipients of grace because we are united to Christ. Because he was raised from the dead, we are raised spiritually now and will be raised physically in the future. Because he is seated and reigning, we are (even now) seated with him and sharing his reign. The Christian faith begins with grace and ends with grace because it begins with Christ and ends with Christ.

APPLY GOD'S WORD

Do you marvel at the display of God's grace? I don't mean: do you marvel at the display of God's grace and glory in his creation? And not: do you marvel at the display of God's grace and glory in the work of others? But do you marvel at the display of God's grace and glory in your life? Do you remember where you came from? Do you recall how you were dead in your trespasses and sins? Can you still envision being led astray by the world, the devil, and the flesh? Are you mindful of how you were deserving of God's wrath?

But then God's grace broke into your life and he saved you, gave life to you, raised you up, and seated you with his beloved Son. Yes, God has displayed his grace and glory in creation and in the lives of others, but he has also displayed his grace and glory in your life. And this is not just an average display but one that shows the immeasurable riches of God's grace. This is a lavish display that should cause our hearts to erupt with praise.

PRAY

Dear God, with the psalmist I cry out, "What is man that you are mindful of him, and the son of man that you care for him?" (Ps 8:4).

I know that it is your grace, and your grace alone, that saves and redeems me. I know that Christ alone has secured my favor with you.

And so, I proclaim, "O Lord, our Lord, how majestic is your name in all the earth!" (Ps 8:9). Amen.

STUDY IT FURTHER

1. Read Romans 6:3–4 and Colossians 2:12, 20; 3:1, which discuss the believer's union with Christ. What concepts are similar to what we find in Ephesians 2:5–7? What concepts are different?

2. In Ephesians 1:20, Paul proclaims that God's mighty power was displayed in Christ "when he raised him from the dead

and seated him at his right hand in the heavenly places." Why do you think that no mention is made of believers being seated at God's "right hand"?

3. In Ephesians 2:7, Paul mentions that God's grace was shown to us "in kindness." What do Romans 2:4 and Titus 3:4 teach us about God's kindness?

Day 11

Ephesians 2:8–10

READ

For by grace you have been saved through faith.
And this is not your own doing; it is the gift of God,
not a result of works, so that no one may
boast. For we are his workmanship, created in
Christ Jesus for good works, which God prepared
beforehand, that we should walk in them.

MEDITATE

This passage represents one of the most well-known and beloved portions of the Bible—and for good reason. Here, Paul emphasizes that salvation is based solely on the undeserved grace of God. After explaining the hopeless situation of how we were dead in our sins and constrained to follow the world, the flesh, and the devil, God's mercy and love breaks into our lives and makes us alive together with Christ. Thus, salvation is solely "by grace." And the grace that results in salvation is received "through faith."

We are saved by grace through faith: Although they might seem somewhat minor, the prepositions used in our English translations are tremendously important. First, when Paul states that we are saved "by grace," the idea is that we are saved *because of,* or *on the basis of,* grace. That is, grace is the basis of our salvation. Second, we are saved "through faith." Faith is the means by which salvation is secured. Note that we are *not* saved because of, or on the basis of, faith. Faith itself does not save but is a conduit or instrument through which we receive God's grace and forgiveness because of Christ's work on the cross. Just as we receive medicine through a syringe, we receive grace (the medicine that saves) through faith (the instrument through which grace flows). We are saved because of the medicine, not because of the syringe. It is only through faith (the syringe), however, that salvation is received. Faith, then, is trusting what Christ has accomplished on our behalf and is not viewed as a meritorious work.

We are not saved by our works: In order to emphasize that our salvation is based on grace and not human effort, Paul adds three qualifying clauses: salvation is (1) "not your own doing," (2) "the gift of God," and (3) "not a result of works" (2:8–9). Paul is emphatically reminding us that the source of salvation does not originate with us; it is a gift of God. A gift by definition is something that is not earned. Both the grace *and* the faith we receive that result in salvation are not of our own doing but are freely given to us by God.

We are saved for good works: Paul also uses new creation language to indicate that salvation is solely of God. Specifically, he states that we are God's "workmanship" (2:10; see also Rom 1:20). This term designates God's work of the new creation (see also Eph 4:24). God not only created us and knit us together in our mothers' wombs, he is responsible for making us a new creation in Christ. We are created for a purpose: we are created for "good works." Paul does not state that our new creation status is *based on* good works. Rather, we are created *for* good works. Our works do not qualify us as worthy of God's favor. If that were the case, who would have hope? Instead, God graciously offers salvation to us because of his great love, which is received by faith.

REFLECT ON CHRIST

Because of his great love and mercy, God extends grace to us. But the grace that is extended to us comes at a cost. To us it is a gift from God that precludes boasting, but to Christ the cost was real. He paid the price with his life on the cross. That is why Paul speaks about boasting only "in the cross of our Lord Jesus Christ" (Gal 6:14). It is free to us, but it comes at a price. Paul reminds us, "You are not your own, for you were bought with a price. So glorify God in your body" (1 Cor 6:19–20).

Paul also informs us that we were created for good works. Note specifically that this new creation life is *in Christ Jesus*. It is because of our union with Christ that we are now able to live a life that is pleasing to God. In other words, we are able to walk in good works because Jesus walked before us. Our good works don't earn us favor with God. We don't work in order to be a new creation. By grace we receive new creation status, and then we respond with good works.

APPLY GOD'S WORD

Because salvation is a free gift of God, boasting is off-limits for us. How can we boast or be arrogant regarding something that comes to us even though we didn't earn it and we don't deserve it? A salvation that is not based on human merit cannot involve human boasting. In Romans 3, after he explains the nature of justification, including how it is not based on works but is a free gift of God, Paul asks, "Then what becomes of our boasting?"

His response, "It is excluded" (v. 27). An arrogant Christian should be an oxymoron.

As Christians, we are not called to boast in our works, but we are called to walk in good works. In Ephesians 2:1–2, Paul explains that prior to faith in Christ we *walked* in our trespasses and sins. In 2:10, Paul indicates that as part of God's re-creation we are called to *walk* in God's preordained good works. Salvation, from beginning to end, is a result of God's grace—even the good works that we perform. And yet, we must strive all the more to walk worthy of our calling. And when we make progress, we proclaim, "Not I, but the grace of God that is with me" (1 Cor 15:10).

PRAY

O Lord, I am prone to rest in my accomplishments
instead of resting in the finished work of Christ.
Forgive me and remind me afresh today that I am wholly
dependent upon your mercy. I humble myself
before you and plead only the blood of Jesus
as a satisfaction for my sins. Help me to walk according
to the good works that you have prepared for me. Amen.

STUDY IT FURTHER

1. Why is it important to know that we are saved on the basis of grace but not on the basis of faith?

2. Because salvation is a gift from God, it excludes all boasting. See Galatians 6:13 and Philippians 3:3 for specific examples of boasting in one's deeds (or flesh). What are deeds that people boast about today?

3. In Ephesians 2:2, Paul indicates that believers formerly walked in their sins following the world, the flesh, and the

devil. Now, however, believers are re-created and called to walk (some translations render it as "live") according to God's ways. Read Ephesians 4:1, 17; 5:2, 8, and 15, and note how Christians are to walk (or not walk).

Day 12

Ephesians 2:11–13

READ

Therefore remember that at one time you Gentiles in the flesh, called "the uncircumcision" by what is called the circumcision, which is made in the flesh by hands— remember that you were at that time separated from Christ, alienated from the commonwealth of Israel and strangers to the covenants of promise, having no hope and without God in the world. But now in Christ Jesus you who once were far off have been brought near by the blood of Christ.

MEDITATE

We are a forgetful people. Just this morning I forgot my phone at home and realized it as I was driving in to work. So, I decided to turn around and get it so that family members and friends could contact me. We forget where we place our keys, glasses, and a hundred other items that seem to mysteriously disappear, only to be found precisely where we placed them.

This passage contains the first explicit command (imperative) in Ephesians and the only one given in the first half (three chapters) of the letter. The command is simple, yet profound: "remember." In particular, Paul exhorts us to remember our past—the condition we were in before coming to saving faith in Christ and consequently being accepted into God's family and receiving all of the accompanying privileges. Remember that at one time we were far from Christ. In 2:12, Paul lists five deficiencies that encapsulate our prior situation.

We were separated from God's Messiah: First, we were "separated from Christ" (the Messiah). The placement of this deficiency at the head of the list indicates that it represents the primary dilemma. Because every spiritual blessing is available only to those united to Christ by faith (1:3–14) and because our rescue from the world, the devil, and the flesh depends on our being united to Christ by faith, then to be without Christ is to forfeit those blessings and status.

We were alienated from God's people: Second, we were "alienated from the commonwealth of Israel." Those of us who are gentiles (that is, all non-Jews) were estranged from God's chosen people and, consequently, all the accompanied privileges of those with citizenship in Israel.

We were strangers to God's covenants: Third, as gentiles, we were "strangers to the covenants of promise." In the Old Testament, God made several covenants (agreements) with his people, including the Abrahamic, Mosaic, Davidic, and new covenants. These covenants included the favor of God and the hope of a coming redeemer (Messiah).

We were without God's hope: Fourth, we had "no hope." Without God, and without a savior, there was no firm foundation on which to base our hope.

We were without God: Finally, we were "without God in the world." Most gentiles in Paul's day would have scoffed at such a notion, since they believed in many gods. But Paul's point is that apart from Christ, no one has a relationship with the true and living God—the God who created heaven and earth, the God who sent his only Son to die on a cross.

But not only are we to remember where we have come from, we are also to remember where we now stand because of God's grace. Because of our union with Christ (Paul's meaning of the phrase "in Christ," 2:13), our status has been changed. We were "once far off" but now "have been brought near" (2:13). What made the difference? How are those who were separated, alienated, strangers, hopeless, and godless now included into the people of God? It is "by the blood of Christ" (2:13). That is, it is through Christ's sacrificial death in our place.

REFLECT ON CHRIST

Once again, we see that Paul is Christ-centered in his understanding of the change that takes place in believers. What was our problem? We were "separated from Christ" (2:12). Being separated from Christ means being separated from the Father. Jesus himself stated, "I am the way, and the truth, and the life. No one comes to the Father except through me" (John 14:6). To be separated from Christ is to be without new life and without hope.

In 2:13, we see a dramatic shift represented by the words "but now." Previously ("at one time," 2:11; "at that time," 2:12), we were far off from God, "but now" we have been brought near. And what made the difference? Again, Paul links our transition to our union with Christ ("in Christ Jesus," 2:13). The only way our circumstances can change, the only way that we are brought near, is through faith and allegiance to the Son of God. But why is it that union with Christ changes our status? It is "by the blood of Christ" (2:13). In his death (and subsequent resurrection), Jesus pays our penalty and secures our place in God's family.

APPLY GOD'S WORD

Are you prone to forget? What did you eat last Tuesday for lunch? What was the passage/topic of the sermon from last Sunday? When was the last time you changed the air filter(s) in your house? We live in a fast-paced, forward-pressing culture. We quickly move on to the next thing before the previous thing has run its course.

We need to force ourselves to slow down and remember. In the Old Testament, the people of Israel were often urged to remember the mighty acts of God, especially how God delivered them from slavery in Egypt (the exodus) and their being brought back into the promised land. The call to remember is not a sterile mental activity. Rather, it is recalling God's past faithfulness in such a way that causes us to live differently. The focus is not gaining new information but reminding ourselves of what we already know so that we are more cognizant of God's faithfulness and grace, which will lead us to respond appropriately. We need to pause regularly and remember God's grace given to us freely through the work of Christ. We were far off but now we are near.

PRAY

Almighty and gracious God, forgive me for my forgetfulness.
I have often forgotten your mercy, love, and grace
that saved me and sustains me. Help me to be mindful
of where I have come from so that I can truly be thankful
for where you have taken me. Thank you for bringing
me near to you through the blood of Christ. Amen.

STUDY IT FURTHER

1. In Deuteronomy, God exhorts the people of Israel to remember their slavery in Egypt and how the Lord redeemed them (see Deut 5:15; 15:15; 16:12; 24:18, 22). In what contexts are the people reminded? For example, Deuteronomy 5:15 is given in the context of the fourth commandment to keep the Sabbath day. Why do you think they are encouraged to "remember" so many times?

2. Paul makes it clear in Ephesians and in other passages that the people of Israel received many blessings as God's covenant people. Read Romans 9:4–5 and note all the blessings given to the Israelites. In the context of Romans 9, how do we know that such privileges did not guarantee salvation?

3. The imagery of being *far* and *near* is not unique to Paul; it can be found in several places in the Old Testament. In Isaiah 57:19 we read, "'Peace, peace, to the far and to the near,' says the LORD, 'and I will heal him.' " Elsewhere, gentiles are described as being "far" (Deut 28:49; 1 Kgs 8:41; Isa 5:26), whereas Israel is described as being "near" (Ps 148:14). Why does Paul use language once applied to Israel for the church?

Day 13

Ephesians 2:14–18

READ

For he himself is our peace, who has made us both one and has broken down in his flesh the dividing wall of hostility by abolishing the law of commandments expressed in ordinances, that he might create in himself one new man in place of the two, so making peace, and might reconcile us both to God in one body through the cross, thereby killing the hostility. And he came and preached peace to you who were far off and peace to those who were near. For through him we both have access in one Spirit to the Father.

MEDITATE

Along with Paul urging us to remember where we have come from (2:11–13), he exhorts us to recall our present situation: that Christ is our peace. In this passage, Paul uses the word "peace" four times (2:14, 15, 17 [x2]), making this the key theme of the passage.

Christ has united both Jew and gentile: First, Christ is our peace because he has made both Jew and gentile one through their mutual faith (2:14). In the place of hostility and discord, Christ has brought peace.

Christ has broken down the dividing wall: Second, Christ is our peace because he has broken down the dividing wall that separated the two groups (2:14). This "wall" is most likely the metaphorical wall of the Mosaic law that divided Jews and gentiles. Laws such as dietary restrictions, Sabbath observance, and circumcision led to a physical separation between the Jewish people and the pagan cultures and religions that surrounded them. It is also possible that the "dividing wall" Paul was referring to was symbolized by the wall around the temple that separated the court of gentiles from the inner courts and the sanctuary. Gentiles could enter into the first section, but the punishment for entering the inner wall for a gentile was death.

Christ has abolished the law: Third, Christ is our peace because he has abolished the law (2:15–16). Here, Paul is not suggesting that the law is useless or destroyed but that the Mosaic law, as part of the Mosaic covenant, has been set aside because it has been fulfilled in Jesus (see Gal 6:2; Heb 7:12). Christ abolished the law for at least two purposes. The first purpose is to create one new man (2:15). Through his death, Christ has recreated a new humanity (see also 2 Cor 5:17; Gal 6:15) where Jew and gentile are brought together as one. When the law is removed and the accompanying hostility that surrounds it, the result is peace. The second purpose for which Jesus set aside the law is so that we might be reconciled to God (2:16). Our peace with others is only possible because we have been reconciled to God. Our unity ("one body") with others was accomplished "though the cross" (2:16).

Christ is the messenger of peace: Fourth, Christ is our peace because he himself is the messenger of peace (2:17–18). He "came and preached peace to you who were far off and peace to those who were near" (2:17). Those "far off" are the gentiles, and "those who were near" are the Jews. The gospel message is a message of peace. It is not only a message of peace and reconciliation with *God*; it is also a message of peace and reconciliation with fallen *humanity*. Jesus provides access to God for both Jews and gentiles. In the Old Testament, access to God was severely restricted. But through Jesus's atoning death and reconciling work, we can freely enter into the presence of God (see Eph 3:12). Notice that all three persons of the Trinity are involved in bringing peace: we have access through Christ, in the Spirit, with the Father.

REFLECT ON CHRIST

Christ is clearly the focus of this passage. He himself is our peace. He made Jews and gentiles one. He has broken down the dividing wall of hostility. He abolished the law of commandments. He created in himself one new humanity. He reconciled us to God through the cross. He killed the hostility. He preached peace to those far and those near. He provided us with access to the Father.

Paul begins this passage by noting that Christ himself is our peace. He is not merely the bringer of peace (though he is that) but is himself peace. Because he is the embodiment of peace, he is the provider of peace—peace with God and peace with others. Gentile believers have been brought near to God "by the blood of Christ" (2:13). The dividing wall has been broken down "in his flesh" (2:14). Unity with God and with humanity was accomplished "through the cross" (2:16). The peace and reconciliation that Christ offers is always tied to his life, death, and resurrection.

APPLY GOD'S WORD

Because of Christ's work, believers are reconciled to God (vertical relationship) and to others (horizontal relationships). It is this horizontal reconciliation that is dominant in this passage. The dividing wall is broken down, creating a united humanity. Racial tension and division run contrary to the nature of the gospel. In Paul's context, this meant that Jewish Christians had no theological justification for rejecting gentiles or for viewing them as outsiders. For gentile Christians, it meant not despising those who were culturally different and rejected by the majority of society.

For us it means that race, ethnicity, or economic status should not divide Christians. According to the apostle John, believers from "every tribe and language and people and nation" (Rev 5:9) will be worshiping around God's throne. When possible, the church should resemble the multitudes worshiping in heaven. Thus, we must labor so that we don't inadvertently contradict the gospel by refusing to worship, fellowship, or serve with people different than ourselves. The gospel gives us the motivation and the power to be united to all believers. Jesus is the prince of peace (Isa 9:6) who has brought peace to his people (John 14:27; Eph 2:17). We need to carry this message of peace and reconciliation to others—a message that is conveyed not only by our words but by our actions.

PRAY

Christ, I thank you that you are my peace. Thank you for your work of reconciliation. It is only through you that I now can have peace with God and peace with others. Help me to bring this message of peace to those both far and near through the strength that you provide. Amen.

STUDY IT FURTHER

1. What does it mean that Christ "abolished" the law (2:15)? How does Romans 3:31 (the same Greek word is translated there "overthrow") help us understand the meaning in Ephesians?

2. Although some have claimed Paul's comments regarding the law are limited to the *ceremonial* and *civil* aspects of the Mosaic law, how do Hebrews 7:12 and Galatians 6:2 suggest that Paul's reference is to the law in its entirety?

3. Read Isaiah 52:7; 57:19. Do you think that Paul's wording is drawn from these passages? If it is, how does this connection help us better understand Paul's comments in Ephesians 2?

Day 14

Ephesians 2:19–22

READ

So then you are no longer strangers and aliens,
but you are fellow citizens with the saints and members
of the household of God, built on the foundation of the
apostles and prophets, Christ Jesus himself being the
cornerstone, in whom the whole structure, being joined
together, grows into a holy temple in the Lord.
In him you also are being built together into
a dwelling place for God by the Spirit.

MEDITATE

Remembering takes effort. Sometimes I leave myself sticky notes so as not to forget something that I need to do. Because we are prone to forget, we are helped by signs that point us back to important realities. Perhaps this is why Paul exhorts us to remember not only where we have come from (2:11–13), and that Christ is our peace (2:14–18), but also our new status in Christ (2:19–22). In order to convey this new status, Paul uses three metaphors—all of which express important truths regarding our new standing in Christ.

God's kingdom: First, we are now citizens in God's kingdom (2:19). Because of Jesus's sacrifice on our behalf, we (specifically gentiles) have been reconciled to God. Consequently, we have gone from being "strangers" to "fellow citizens." A *stranger* is a person from a different tribe or country. Earlier, Paul used the term to describe gentiles as those who were "strangers to the covenants of promise" (2:12). Thus, we who were once considered foreigners and outsiders are now accepted as citizens of God's kingdom. In Philippians 3:20, Paul likewise states that "our citizenship is in heaven" (see also Gal 4:6).

God's household: Second, we are now members of God's household (2:19). Because of Jesus's work of reconciliation, we are no longer "aliens" but are "members of the household of God." An *alien* is someone who resides in a land as a temporary guest, not a permanent resident. As such, they do not possess the rights and privileges of citizens and remain outsiders. But through Christ, we have been brought into God's family—we are part of his household. Our adoption has granted us all the rights, privileges, and responsibilities of an heir (see also Eph 1:5; 2:18). Our heavenly Father receives us as his children and will protect and provide for us.

God's temple: Third, we are now part of God's holy temple (2:20–22). Because of Christ's reconciling work, we are described as building stones in the place where God dwells—his temple. This temple is built by God on the foundation of the authoritative and normative teaching of the apostles and prophets (2:20) with Jesus Christ as the cornerstone. Furthermore, this temple is currently under construction, because it is growing both spiritually (into a *holy* temple) and numerically (as gentile believers are added). Perhaps the most remarkable feature of this temple is that it is the dwelling place of God (2:22). In the Old Testament, God's presence was uniquely located in the temple. Now, because of our union with Christ and the indwelling of God's Spirit, together as the family of God, we are the temple of God. Our status has been changed. We went from being Christ-less, homeless, friendless, hopeless, and godless to being citizens, family members, and God's dwelling place.

REFLECT ON CHRIST

Paul indicates that Christ Jesus is the cornerstone of God's temple—the most important stone that bore the weight of the building, tying the walls firmly together. In the New Testament, the term "cornerstone" only occurs twice: here in Ephesians 2:20 and in 1 Peter 2:6 where we read, "Behold, I am laying in Zion a stone, a cornerstone chosen and precious, and whoever believes in him will not be put to shame." It is likely that both Paul and Peter are alluding to the only place where that term is used in the Old Testament—Isaiah 28:16: "Therefore thus says the Lord God, 'Behold, I am the one who has laid as a foundation in Zion, a stone, a tested stone, a precious cornerstone, of a sure foundation.' " Paul's point is clear: Jesus is the most important part of God's building.

This temple only consists of those who are united with Christ through faith. Though subtle, this truth is highlighted twice in our passage. In verse 21 Paul uses "in whom," and in verse 22 he writes "in him." Both of these phrases are references to Christ and the believer's union with him. The only access into God's family and being part of God's dwelling place is through our faith and allegiance to the Son of God.

APPLY GOD'S WORD

It's hard to change the way we think. We are creatures of habit, and once a pattern is established, it becomes difficult to break. Paul exhorts us not only to think about the past (our former life apart from Christ) and the peace we now have but to recall our new status. We are now citizens in God's kingdom (with new privileges and responsibilities), members of God's household (no longer foreigners), and part of God's holy temple (the very place where God dwells). In one sense, these are hidden realities. We cannot see God's kingdom in its fullness. We cannot see that we are now part of God's household and given the full status as his children. We cannot see God's temple and the Spirit residing in us.

But in another sense, we can see the effects of those realities. God's kingdom is growing, and with eyes of faith we can see it expand. We experience life together with those in our local congregations, those who now are our brothers and sisters in the faith. We can see the Spirit move among us as we become more Christlike (the fruit of the Spirit), and we can experience being filled with the Spirit. It is not always easy to see these realities, but that is why we take time to remember the saving grace of the one to whom we belong.

PRAY

O God, open the eyes of my heart so that I can see as you see. Reading that I am now part of your kingdom, household, and temple is easier than truly believing it. O Lord, I believe, but help my unbelief. In Christ I am a kingdom citizen, family member, and the dwelling place of your Spirit. Amen.

STUDY IT FURTHER

1. Who are the apostles and prophets that Paul mentions? Some have suggested that Paul is referring to New Testament apostles and Old Testament prophets. Do you think the word order here ("apostles and prophets" instead

of "prophets and apostles") suggests that Paul has New Testament prophets in mind?

2. According to Old Testament prophecy, at the end times, the nations will come to the temple in Jerusalem to worship the living God (see Isa 2:1–5; 66:18–20; Mic 4:1–5). In using this temple imagery, could Paul be suggesting that these promises are being fulfilled as gentiles place their faith in Christ and, with believing Jews, become the new temple of God?

3. Read 1 Corinthians 3:16–17 and 2 Corinthians 6:16. What do these passages teach us about the temple of God?

Day 15

Ephesians 3:1–7

READ

For this reason I, Paul, a prisoner of Christ Jesus on behalf of you Gentiles—assuming that you have heard of the stewardship of God's grace that was given to me for you, how the mystery was made known to me by revelation, as I have written briefly. When you read this, you can perceive my insight into the mystery of Christ, which was not made known to the sons of men in other generations as it has now been revealed to his holy apostles and prophets by the Spirit. This mystery is that the Gentiles are fellow heirs, members of the same body, and partakers of the promise in Christ Jesus through the gospel. Of this gospel I was made a minister according to the gift of God's grace, which was given me by the working of his power.

MEDITATE

We often talk about God's will for our lives in terms of a location or a vocation, but the Bible often speaks about God's will in terms of obedience to God's commands (see Gal 5:13; Eph

4:1; 1 Thess 4:7; 1 Pet 2:21; 3:9). For Paul, obedience to God's commands led him to be locked up in Nero's prison. In this passage, Paul identifies himself as a "prisoner of Jesus Christ" (3:1). Notice that Paul does not describe himself as a prisoner of Nero Caesar but of Jesus Christ. More specifically, he is a prisoner "on behalf of you Gentiles" (3:1). That is, Paul's incarceration is directly linked to the fulfilling of his apostolic calling of preaching the gospel to gentiles. Paul's calling was to preach the gospel, and obedience to that calling sometimes led him to persecution and imprisonment. God's will for our lives is to obey his commands and his calling. We don't always know where that will lead, but we can be certain that it is part of his plan.

Paul was a steward of God's grace: God's plan for Paul included him being a steward of God's grace. As mentioned above, Paul's stewardship (i.e., his calling) included the responsibility of proclaiming the good news of Jesus to the nations. Paul refers to God's plan for humanity as a "mystery" (3:3, 4, 6). This term refers to God's plan to unite both Jews and gentiles into the one people of God through Christ. Paul emphasizes that his calling to proclaim this message is not something he conceived but a part of God's plan. Twice Paul remarks that his stewardship of God's grace "was given" to him (3:2, 7). This passive construction leaves out the implied subject, which is none other than God himself—the one who gave. Paul received his message and his mission "by revelation" (3:3). God revealed to Paul this understanding, probably referring to his Damascus road experience. Finally, Paul was granted insight into this special revelation from God.

Paul was given insight into God's plan of salvation: The insight into the mystery that Paul received involved something previously unknown. But now, through his Spirit, God has revealed the nature of this mystery to the apostles and prophets—including to Paul himself. This does not mean that God's plan to include the gentiles was completely unknown in the Old Testament. Rather, there was no clear indication that Jews and gentiles would be united to form the one people of God as the body of Christ. When describing the content of the mystery, Paul employs three terms to signify the relationship of gentiles with Jews. They are "fellow heirs, members of the same body, and partakers of the promise" (3:6). Paul concludes by stating that he was made a minister of the gospel, again demonstrating that this appointment was not of Paul's choosing but a part of God's plan. Paul sees himself merely as a servant who is a recipient of God's grace. God's will for Paul was for him to obey his commands. God's calling involved him preaching the gospel to the nations, a calling that involved persecution, suffering, imprisonment, and ultimately death.

REFLECT ON CHRIST

Once again, we see that Christ is central to this passage. First, Paul is a prisoner of Jesus Christ (3:1). He was willing to suffer as a condemned criminal for the sake of his Lord, who himself suffered as a condemned criminal. Second, Paul describes the mystery as the "mystery of Christ" (3:4), which most likely means that it is a mystery *about* Christ. That is, Christ is the focus and center of God's plan to redeem Jews and gentiles and unite them together into one body. Third, the threefold blessings that gentiles receive are given precisely because of union with Christ (3:6). Namely, gentiles are now *fellow heirs* (3:6), which recalls the theme of inheritance found earlier in Ephesians (1:11, 14, 18) and harkens back to God's promise to Abraham that "in you all the families of the earth shall be blessed" (Gen 12:3). Additionally, the gentiles are now "members of the same body" or *fellow members* who have been united and have become "one new man" (Eph 2:15) or "one body" (2:16). Finally, gentiles are *fellow partakers* of the promise in Christ Jesus, a promise that refers to the Holy Spirit (see 1:13), or the blessings that would come to the gentiles mentioned in God's promise to Abraham, or both. All of these blessings are based on union with Christ since it is only through faith in Christ and his life, death, resurrection, and ascension that these blessings can be attained.

APPLY GOD'S WORD

Paul suffered while obeying God's plan for his life as an apostle to the gentiles. He tells the Ephesians that he suffered for them and sought to encourage them in the midst of his imprisonment. Although we might expect that Paul would be the one in need of encouragement, he is the one encouraging the Ephesians. He was under house arrest, chained to a Roman soldier, and upon the precipice of death. And yet, even in the midst of his suffering, he was faithfully preaching the gospel to those in prison and to the prison guards. He was declaring the gospel by writing letters to the churches in Ephesus, Philippi, and Colossae.

How do you look at suffering in your life? True, sometimes we suffer because of poor decisions we make, but we can also suffer when we are doing precisely what God has called us to do. Just as God fulfilled his purposes through Paul's suffering, he also fulfills his purposes through our suffering. Paul was not a prisoner of Nero but a prisoner of Jesus Christ. Let us be faithful to what God has called us to do and trust that God is sovereignly working out all things for good for those who love him.

PRAY

Father in heaven, help me to trust in your goodness and kindness, even in the midst of suffering. Just as you used the suffering of the apostle Paul, as well as the saints who came before and after him, use me for your glory. Thank you for allowing me to be part of your divine plan. Amen.

STUDY IT FURTHER

1. Paul states that he received "insight" into the mystery of Christ (3:4). This expression is frequently found in the Old Testament, especially in relation to Daniel and his ability to understand and interpret the revelation of God as mediated through dreams and visions. Read Daniel 1:4, 17; 9:13, 23; 10:1, 11. How is Paul's insight similar to that of Daniel, and how is it different?

2. God's plan for including the gentiles into the people of God is called a mystery. Yet not everything related to their reception into the people of God is foreign to the Old Testament (see Gen 12:3; 22:18; 26:4; 28:14). What blessings were prophesied to come to the gentiles?

3. Read Isaiah 32:15; 44:3; Ezekiel 11:19; 36:26–27; 37:14; and Joel 2:28–29. When the gentiles are called fellow "partakers of the promise in Christ Jesus," do you think this refers to both the promise of the Holy Spirit *and* the blessings to the gentiles in the Abrahamic covenant (see Rom 4:13; Gal 3:8)? Why or why not?

Day 16

Ephesians 3:8–13

READ

To me, though I am the very least of all the saints,
this grace was given, to preach to the Gentiles
the unsearchable riches of Christ, and to bring to light for
everyone what is the plan of the mystery hidden for ages in
God, who created all things, so that through the church
the manifold wisdom of God might now
be made known to the rulers and authorities
in the heavenly places. This was according to the eternal
purpose that he has realized in Christ Jesus our Lord,
in whom we have boldness and access with confidence
through our faith in him. So I ask you not to lose heart
over what I am suffering for you, which is your glory.

MEDITATE

This passage continues many of the themes found in the previous passage (3:1–7), but we will shift our focus from emphasizing Paul's calling and how obedience to that calling led to suffering to considering Paul's specific calling to preach the gospel of Jesus Christ and how God uses the church to display his wisdom.

Paul was an unworthy servant of God: Paul considered himself unworthy to be a servant of God. First, Paul declares once again that the grace to preach *was given* to him. He didn't earn it or deserve it. It was something God graciously bestowed upon him. Second, he describes himself as "the very least of all the saints" (3:8). In 1 Corinthians 15:9, Paul declares himself to be the least of all the apostles, but here he broadens the scope to all the saints. Third, Paul was suffering (3:13). Some would have viewed such suffering as a sign of divine disfavor. But Paul knew the very reason he was suffering as a prisoner of Christ was because of his calling to preach the gospel.

Paul was tasked to preach the gospel to the gentiles: God's grace is what enabled Paul to fulfill his ministry of preaching the gospel. More specifically, this grace was given to Paul "to preach to the Gentiles" (3:8). What did Paul preach to them? He preached "the unsearchable riches of Christ" (3:8). The only other occurrence of the term "unsearchable" in the New Testament is found in Romans 11:33, where Paul exclaims: "Oh, the depth of the riches and wisdom and knowledge of God! How *unsearchable* are his judgments and how inscrutable his ways!" (emphasis added). Paul further clarifies that grace was given to him "to bring to light for everyone what is the plan of the mystery" (Eph 3:9). He was commissioned to preach the gospel to the nations and reveal God's mystery. As Paul preached the unsearchable riches of Christ in the gospel, those who repented and believed were brought into God's family.

Paul further clarifies that the purpose he preached is "so that ... the manifold wisdom of God might now be made known" (3:10). God's wisdom, which is displayed in the gospel of Jesus Christ, surpasses all other wisdom and knowledge. Paul can confidently proclaim this divine message because it is "according to the eternal purpose" of God (3:11). The mystery that was hidden to previous generations but is now revealed was part of God's intention from all eternity. What is the result of those who trust in this glorious gospel? We have "boldness and access with confidence" (3:12) to enter into God's presence. That is, we have privileged and certain access to God and can approach him without fear of being rejected. Instead, we can have great confidence that God will receive us because of the perfect and complete work of Christ on our behalf.

Discouragement often comes when we don't get our way. But Paul believed that his suffering was a part of God's plan and that God was using him even in prison. He shared his experience of suffering because he wanted his readers to trust in God and not to lose heart.

REFLECT ON CHRIST

Christ is referenced four times in this passage. First, the message that Paul preached focused on "the unsearchable riches of Christ" (3:8). The word translated "unsearchable" could also be rendered "inscrutable" or "incomprehensible." It refers to something that is impossible to fully comprehend even after careful examination. The irony is that Paul's preaching sought to make known that which is ultimately unknowable. There is always more to know and appreciate regarding Christ and his sacrifice for us.

Second, Paul revealed God's purpose, which was "realized in Christ Jesus our Lord" (3:11). That is, the purpose or plan that God has always intended has now been accomplished in Christ Jesus. Although God's purposes are not fully complete, they are now guaranteed because of the perfect and complete work of Christ. Jesus's mission was to fulfill the will of his Father, which not only led him to the cross but secured his resurrection and ascension to the Father's right hand.

Third, Paul indicates that we have boldness and can confidently access the Father because of our union with Christ. In 3:12, the phrase "in whom" is a reference to Christ. Fourth, Christ is the object of the believer's faith. Paul states that our boldness to enter God's presence is "through our faith in him" (3:12), another reference to Christ. Our acceptance before God is based on Christ's reconciling work, and it is through faith in him that we acquire the privilege of approaching his throne of grace freely.

APPLY GOD'S WORD

The church, by its very existence as a multiracial community of Jews and gentiles, is a declaration of God's wisdom to the world. Paul writes that it is "through the church the manifold wisdom of God might now be made known" (3:10). The church is not an addendum in God's plan but an integral part of his eternal purpose. From the beginning, God sought to make his wisdom known through the church. This incredible mystery that was once hidden has now been revealed through the apostles and prophets—a mystery that focuses on Christ and his church. Through his Son, God has created a new people consisting of both Jews and gentiles. This redeemed community (the church) is united by its common faith in the Messiah. The church is made up of people from various races and cultures who, because of their union with Christ, all enjoy a relationship with the Father and have been adopted as his children. How does your walk with Christ reflect that you are part of a multiracial, redeemed community that forms God's holy habitation?

PRAY

O God, give me boldness and confidence
to enter your presence through the work of Christ
in the power of the Holy Spirit.
Give me the boldness of Paul to make known
the unsearchable riches of Christ. Give me confidence
in your plan to bring all races together in Christ. Amen.

STUDY IT FURTHER

1. Paul calls himself "the very least of all the saints" (Eph 3:8), "the least of the apostles" (1 Cor 15:9), and the "foremost" of sinners (1 Tim 1:15). Do you think Paul was exaggerating? In what way are these labels true of us?

2. The term "boldness" (3:12), sometimes translated "confidence," conveys the idea of the freedom to speak freely and openly. Read Hebrews 4:16 and 10:19 and reflect on the amazing freedom and permission believers are granted.

3. The verb translated "lose heart" (3:13) could similarly be rendered "lose enthusiasm" or "be discouraged."[1] Compare how Paul uses the term here to the other uses of the term in the New Testament (Luke 18:1; 2 Cor 4:1, 16; Gal 6:9; and 2 Thess 3:13). Why do you think that believers are tempted to "lose heart"?

1. Walter Bauer, Frederick Danker, William F. Arndt, and F. Wilbur Gingrich, *A Greek-English Lexicon of the New Testament and Other Early Christian Literature*, 3rd ed. (University of Chicago, 2002), 272.

Day 17

Ephesians 3:14–19

READ

For this reason I bow my knees before the Father,
from whom every family in heaven and on earth is named,
that according to the riches of his glory he may grant you
to be strengthened with power through his Spirit
in your inner being, so that Christ may dwell
in your hearts through faith—that you, being rooted
and grounded in love, may have strength to comprehend
with all the saints what is the breadth and length and height
and depth, and to know the love of Christ that surpasses
knowledge, that you may be filled with all the fullness of God.

MEDITATE

Paul was a man of prayer. His commitment to prayer is seen in his admonitions for others to pray (e.g., 1 Thess 5:17) and in the prayers he offers in his letters. This passage records his second prayer for the Ephesians (see 1:15–22). In this prayer, Paul offers three requests to the Father on behalf of his readers: strengthening, understanding, and filling.

A prayer for strengthening: First, Paul asks that we may be strengthened so that Christ dwells in our hearts (3:16–17). This request acknowledges our dependence on God. We need strength from an outside source. We are not sufficient on our own. We need the power and strength that come from God. In his first prayer, Paul implores his readers to have their hearts enlightened to know "what is the immeasurable greatness of his power" (1:18), but here he prays they would be recipients of that power and strength. This strength that God supplies is given "according to the riches of his glory" (3:16). The resources of God available to us are limitless. Thus, God will lavishly provide all the strength we need (see Phil 4:19). The result of God strengthening us is "that Christ may dwell in [our] hearts" (3:17). Although Christ indwells the hearts of believers through the Spirit from conversion, here Paul is referring to Christ's continual indwelling influence, which is attained through the active faith of a believer in the finished and perfect work of Christ.

A prayer for understanding: Second, Paul prays the Ephesians may have the strength to understand or comprehend the love of Christ (3:17–19). Paul begins this request by mentioning the necessity of "being rooted and grounded in love" (3:17). God's love for us provides the basis and motivating strength that enables us to love others. The heart of Paul's request is that we will be able to grasp the immense love of Christ for us. This love is described with physical dimensions (breadth, length, height, and depth), which convey the immensity of Christ's love for us (see also Rom 8:35–36). This grasping of Christ's all-encompassing love is not for a few select believers but for "all the saints." Paul wants us to be empowered to comprehend the incomprehensible love that Christ has for us. He prays we will be able to know the love which "surpasses knowledge" (3:19).

A prayer for filling: Third, Paul requests that the believers be filled with all the fullness of God (3:19). Many of us are full of ourselves, meaning we are arrogant or prideful. But Paul prays that we may be filled with God and the love we receive from him. Later in Ephesians, Paul writes that believers are to attain "to the measure of the stature of the fullness of Christ" (4:13). The meaning of "fullness" in these passages most likely refers to God's moral excellence or perfections, especially his love. Thus, Paul is praying that we would comprehend Christ's love for us and that God would fill us so that we attain his perfections, especially love.

REFLECT ON CHRIST

Similar to how Jesus taught us to pray (e.g., Matt 6:9), Paul addresses God as Father. In the New Testament, prayers are consistently offered to God the Father, but in Paul's prayer, he mentions Christ twice—once in each of the first two requests. In the first reference, he asks that "Christ may dwell" in our hearts through faith (3:17). The verb "dwell" indicates a permanent indwelling and not just a temporary residence. The phrase "in your hearts" (3:17) is parallel to "in your inner being" (3:16) and indicates that the Spirit of Christ indwells the very center of our being.

In his second reference, Paul prays that we may know "the love of Christ." This phrase could refer to our love for Christ or to Christ's love for us. In this context, Paul clearly intends the second option, which is consistent with other uses of the phrase. In Romans 8:35, Paul asks, "Who shall separate us from the love of Christ?" and in 2 Corinthians 5:14, he remarks, "The love of Christ controls us." These passages could be rendered, "Who shall separate us from Christ's love for us?" and "Christ's love for us controls us." It is when Christ dwells in us that we begin to comprehend his love for us.

APPLY GOD'S WORD

This prayer reminds us that we are not powerful in and of ourselves. The rugged individualism, self-help, or do-it-yourself mentality of our culture can easily lead us astray. In order to love and serve God, resist the temptations of the world, the devil, and the flesh, and bring the name of Christ to a lost and dying world, we must rely on God's strength and not our own.

This prayer also reminds us of Christ's immense love for his people. This love cannot be measured because it has no limits. Earlier in Ephesians, Paul reminds us that, before he created the heavens and the earth, God chose us "in love" (1:4). Although we were dead in our trespasses and sins, God made us alive "because of the great love with which he loved us" (2:4). This love surpasses our ability to fully comprehend its magnitude. And God's great power ensures that his immense love will never fail.

Finally, this prayer reminds us that God dwells with and in his people. John reminds us that "God is light, and in him is no darkness at all" (1 John 1:5). We should, therefore, seek to be a holy habitation where God dwells. As a result of God's presence, we are filled with God's fullness and experience his power and love.

PRAY

Holy Father, help me to rely on the strength that you supply so that in everything you may be glorified through Jesus Christ (1 Pet 4:11). Help me to comprehend Christ's love for me, which he displayed most clearly by his sacrifice on my behalf. O God, fill me with your presence this day. Amen.

STUDY IT FURTHER

1. Paul often testified to how the Lord strengthened him. He also encouraged others to find their strength in God. Read Ephesians 6:10; 1 Timothy 1:12; 2 Timothy 2:2; and 4:17, and write down how these verses encourage you to look to God for strength.

2. The verb "dwell" (3:17) is also found in Ephesians 2:22; Colossians 1:19; and 2:9. Read these passages and note whether or not this indwelling represents a permanent or temporary residence.

3. In the Old Testament, God's presence filled the tabernacle and the temple. Earlier in Ephesians, Paul indicates that both Jewish and gentile believers are "a holy temple" (2:21). How does God's indwelling of believers relate to how we should live (see also 4:22–24)?

Day 18

Ephesians 3:20–21

READ

Now to him who is able to do far more abundantly
than all that we ask or think, according to the power
at work within us, to him be glory
in the church and in Christ Jesus
throughout all generations, forever and ever. Amen.

MEDITATE

After praying for the Ephesian believers (3:14–19), Paul bursts out with a doxology. The term "doxology" comes from the Greek word meaning "glory" or "honor." It is a short hymn of praise to God for who he is and what he has done. Not only is this doxology a fitting conclusion to Paul's prayer, it is an appropriate conclusion for the first half of Paul's letter. A doxology typically contains three parts: (1) a description of the one receiving the praise; (2) a declaration of praise; and (3) the duration of how long such praise should be given.

Description of the recipient of praise: In the first part, Paul provides a description of the one receiving the praise (3:20). He begins by addressing God as the powerful one ("to him who is able") who can accomplish more than what we can even imagine ("to do far more abundantly than all that we ask or think"). Paul emphasizes the power of God with the use of "him who is able" (which could be rendered "him who is powerful") and then adds that all things are accomplished "according to the power" that God is working within us. It is one thing to state that God is powerful enough to do *all* that we imagine. It is another thing to state that he can do *more than* we imagine. Paul takes it a step further by writing that God is able (and willing) to do *far more abundantly than* we ask or imagine. Paul uses a rare adjective (*hyperekperissou*) that means "quite beyond all measure" and communicates "the highest form of comparison imaginable."[2] Paul's previous prayer—that God would strengthen us in our inner being, grant us understanding to comprehend the love of Christ, and fill us with the fullness of God—may seem overly bold and ambitious. Did Paul ask too much in his prayer? This verse gives us the answer: God is able to do this and even more.

Declaration of praise: The second part of the doxology is the declaration of praise, where God is ascribed glory, honor, and power. God does not need our praise. When we offer praise to him or give him glory, we are not giving him something that he does not already possess. We are simply praising him for who he is and what he has done. We are joining the chorus of the hosts of heaven, who continually cry out, "Holy, holy, holy, is the Lord God almighty" (Rev 4:8). God's glory is seen "in the church" through the unity of Jew and gentile as the body of Christ and "in Christ Jesus" who is the head of the church and the one who has united the people of God (3:21).

---

2. Walter Bauer, Frederick Danker, William F. Arndt, and F. Wilbur Gingrich, *A Greek-English Lexicon of the New Testament and Other Early Christian Literature*, 3rd ed. (University of Chicago, 2002), 1033.

Duration of praise: The final part of the doxology provides the duration of how long praise should be given: "throughout all generations, forever and ever" (3:21). That is, God should be praised forever, without end, throughout all eternity. Paul ends the doxology with the familiar term "amen," which can be translated, "Let it be so."

REFLECT ON CHRIST

In this doxology, Paul offers praise to God the Father since he is worthy of all our adoration and devotion. When Paul speaks of the power of God at work within us (3:20), it is this same power that raised Jesus from the dead and exalted him to the Father's side above all other powers (see 1:20).

Paul declares that glory is to be given to God both in "the church" and "in Christ Jesus" (3:21). Once again, we see that God's glory is revealed in his Son. The position of Christ's name directly after the reference to the church demonstrates their close connection. Every spiritual blessing available to us is because we are "in Christ" (1:3–14). The church is the body of Christ, and the Father has given the Son "as head over all things to the church" (1:22–23). Gentiles are brought near to God and to God's people because of their union with Christ (2:13). The dividing wall of hostility is broken down and peace is restored because of Christ's work (2:14–17). We have access to the Father and are no longer strangers and foreigners but members of God's household because we are united to Christ (2:18–19). Christ is the chief cornerstone of the church (2:20–22). Thus, God's glory is clearly seen in Christ and his relationship to the church.

APPLY GOD'S WORD

Paul describes God as one who is able and powerful. Is that your view of God? The reason Paul erupts with praise is because he has a clear understanding of who God is. God created all things by his powerful word (Heb 1:3). He chooses us, redeems us, provides an inheritance for us, and seals us with his Spirit (Eph 1:3–14). He raised Jesus from the dead (1:20). He raised us to new life and seated us with Christ in the heavenly places (2:4–7). And he unites Jews and gentiles (2:11–22). This God is worthy of our praise.

Paul also mentions that God is able to do abundantly far more than we ask. In what areas is it hard to trust God with your requests? How can you trust in God's power and plan when the answer seems unclear to your prayers? Some of the issues we might pray for may seem impossible, but with God's intervening grace and power, he can do all things, even when his response might not look like how we expect him to answer our prayers.

PRAY

Lord, help me to believe that you are able to do
far more abundantly than all that we ask or think,
according to the power at work within us. And I pray
with Paul that you may be glorified
in the church and in Christ Jesus throughout
all generations, forever and ever. Amen.

STUDY IT FURTHER

1. Read the doxologies found in Romans 16:25–27; 1 Timothy 1:17; and Jude 24–25. How are these doxologies similar to and different from the one found in Ephesians 3:20–21?

2. What do you notice about the placement of these doxologies in the contexts of the letters in which they are found?

3. What do these doxologies teach us about God?

Day 19

Ephesians 4:1–3

READ

I therefore, a prisoner for the Lord, urge you to walk in a
manner worthy of the calling
to which you have been called,
with all humility and gentleness, with patience,
bearing with one another in love, eager to maintain
the unity of the Spirit in the bond of peace.

MEDITATE

This passage represents a shift in the letter. After providing the theological foundations for how we came to new life (because of God's love, Christ's sacrifice, and the Spirit's empowerment), Paul now exhorts us to live a life that is worthy of our calling. The main focus of this passage is found in the phrase "I … urge you to walk" (4:1). The theme of walking continues throughout this letter (mentioned at least four more times, 4:17; 5:2, 8, 15). Paul uses it as a metaphor for someone's conduct or way of life. But precisely how should we walk? Paul provides the virtues of our calling and then the values of our calling.

The virtues of our calling: First, Paul lists three virtues that represent what it means for us to walk worthy of our calling: humility, gentleness, and patience (4:2). With the emphasis on unity in this section (4:1–6), it is not difficult to understand why Paul stresses the need for *humility*. Pride and arrogance destroy unity. In order for God's people to be unified, humility must be present. Peter states, "God opposes the proud but gives grace to the humble" (1 Pet 5:5). Indeed, Jesus is our example of humility (see Phil 2:1–11). Paul includes *gentleness* as part of the fruit of the Spirit (Gal 5:23), and it is a crucial quality needed when restoring someone who has sinned (Gal 6:1) and for correcting those who propagate false teachings (2 Tim 2:25). *Patience* is a virtue often tied to God (see Exod 34:6). God's patience is what leads us to repentance (Rom 2:4) because he does not want anyone to perish (2 Pet 3:9). Patience is also a fruit of the Spirit (Gal 5:22), a defining quality of love (1 Cor 13:4), and a virtue that believers are to show to each other (Col 3:12; 1 Thess 5:14; 2 Tim 4:2).

The values of our calling: Paul presents two ways in which we are called to live out our calling. First, we must "[bear] with one another in love" (4:2). Paul is not merely suggesting that we tolerate one another. Rather, we must interact with one another "in love" or lovingly (see also Col 3:13). Second, we walk in a manner worthy of our calling when we are "eager to maintain the unity of the Spirit" (Eph 4:3). Notice that Paul does not simply state we should seek to maintain unity. He adds we should be "eager" to do so, a term that adds a sense of urgency. We are also not urged to *create* unity. Rather, we are exhorted to *maintain* a unity that already exists because of the unifying work of Christ, who broke down the dividing wall of hostility and created a new humanity (2:11–22). Furthermore, this unity is linked to the Spirit since the Spirit is the source of all true unity. Thus, we are urged to maintain the unity that has been attained by Christ and is given by the Spirit—a unity that is held together by peace.

REFLECT ON CHRIST

Christ is specifically mentioned once in this passage, when Paul identifies himself as "a prisoner for the Lord" (4:1; see also 3:1). Paul's references to the "Lord" consistently refer to Jesus in Ephesians, and this verse is no exception. Perhaps by calling himself a prisoner of the Lord Jesus, Paul is adding authority to his following appeal.

It is significant that the commands of conduct follow calling. In other words, the power to live a new life (conduct) only comes after the regenerating power of God and the indwelling of God's Spirit (calling). We don't live worthily to be accepted by God, but having been accepted by God, we now seek to live in a way worthy of our calling. To get this wrong is to get the gospel wrong and to misunderstand Jesus's sacrifice.

Jesus is our prime example of the virtues and values of our calling. Jesus displays perfect humility (Phil 2:1–11), gentleness (Matt 11:29; 2 Cor 10:1), and patience (see Jesus's interactions with his hard-hearted disciples). Christ also exhibited the values of bearing with others (Matt 17:17) and unifying God's people (Eph 2:11–22; John 17:22–23).

APPLY GOD'S WORD

Christians have a high calling. We are called to be holy because God is holy (1 Pet 1:16). We are called to follow the example of Christ, who perfectly obeyed God's law, even in the midst of suffering and persecution. We are called to be humble, gentle, and patient. We are called to lovingly bear with others and to eagerly maintain unity. This list sounds overwhelming since none of us measures up to this high standard.

There are at least two ways we can (and should) respond to this dilemma. First, knowing your failings and sin, look to Christ. We continually sin and fall short of the glory of God. Christ provided atonement for all our sins: past, present, and future. His sacrifice was sufficient and effective to cover our sin and bring us into a right relationship with God.

Second, we can seek to live a more virtuous life by the power of the Spirit. Which virtue mentioned in today's passage is difficult for you to exhibit? Read and meditate on passages that highlight that virtue. Memorize Scripture related to that virtue and commit to praying for strength to improve in that virtue.

PRAY

God, thank you for your mercy and grace that you freely give to us because of your Son, Jesus Christ. Help me be more humble, more gentle, and more patient. And help me to be more tolerant with others and to actively seek to unify your people. Amen.

STUDY IT FURTHER

1. The conjunction "therefore" (4:1) refers back to the first half of the letter. Paul is declaring that, based on the truths of chapters 1–3, we ought to live a certain way. See Paul's use of this conjunction in Romans 12:1; Colossians 3:1 (translated "then"); and 1 Thessalonians 4:1. Does it function in the same way?

2. The theme of walking is prominent in Ephesians 4 and 5 (see 4:1, 17; 5:2, 8, 15). List all the ways that Paul instructs believers to walk in these passages.

3. The term "to be eager" or "do one's best" (*spoudadzō*) is used by Paul to communicate intense effort and labor, often in connection with Paul's travels (see 1 Thess 2:17, "we endeavored ... eagerly"; 2 Tim 4:9, "Do your best"; 4:21, "Do your best"; Titus 3:12, "Do your best"). It is also used by Peter in 2 Peter 1:10 ("be ... diligent") and 3:14 ("be diligent"). How do these passages shed light on the meaning of the term in Ephesians 4:3?

Day 20

Ephesians 4:4–6

READ

There is one body and one Spirit—
just as you were called to the one hope that belongs
to your call—one Lord, one faith, one baptism,
one God and Father of all,
who is over all and through all and in all.

MEDITATE

Unity is something we all appreciate but not something we all facilitate. In other words, on paper, we all would say yes to unity, but oftentimes we are unwilling to take the necessary steps to secure unity. As we saw in the previous passage, unity requires certain virtues (humility, gentleness, and patience) along with certain values (loving tolerance and eagerly seeking peace). But Paul also reminds us of the foundation of unity. What is it that makes our unity so necessary? In this passage, Paul offers a sevenfold answer to that question.

One body: First, we should seek unity because there is "one body" (4:4). The body that Paul is referring to is the body of Christ (see 1:22–23). It is not by accident that Paul mentions the singularity of the church first since it is the focus of the apostle's concern. Although the church consists of many members with various gifts, they compose one body.

One Spirit: Second, we should seek unity because there is "one Spirit" (Eph 4:4; see also 1 Cor 12:11, 13). Not only are believers sealed with the Spirit (Eph 1:13), granted access to the Father through the Spirit (2:18), a dwelling place for God by the Spirit (2:22), and strengthened in the inner person through the Spirit (3:16), but the Spirit is who unifies believers in one body.

One hope: Third, we should seek unity because there is "one hope" to which we have been called (4:4). The calling that we receive is linked to hope. This hope is not the subjective feeling we experience one moment and is gone the next. Rather, it is the objective content of the truths of the gospel that never change.

One Lord: Fourth, we should seek unity because there is "one Lord" (4:5). There is no doubt that this refers to Jesus Christ since God the Father is mentioned in the following verse. This claim of one Lord was a bold statement in a cultural context that proclaimed Caesar or Artemis of Ephesus as "Lord."

One faith: Fifth, we should seek unity because there is "one faith" (4:5). The term "faith" here does not refer to a person's act of belief but to the content of what a person believes. That is, it is the body of belief that we affirm.

One baptism: Sixth, we should seek unity because there is "one baptism" (4:5). The physical act of water baptism is a symbol of the Spirit baptizing the believer at conversion. It represents the initiation and inclusion into the people of God (i.e., the one body).

One God and Father: Seventh, we should seek unity because there is "one God and Father of all" (4:6). This statement is reminiscent of the Old Testament Shema: "Hear, O Israel: The

Lord our God, the Lord is one" (Deut 6:4). Because God is both transcendent (he is "over all") and immanent (he is "through all and in all"), he is not only sovereign over his creation, he is present with his creation. Consequently, we are united together with other believers through our common Father.

REFLECT ON CHRIST

This passage highlights Jesus by reminding us that there is "one Lord" (4:5). In the Old Testament, God was often referred to as "Lord." As we have already noted, Deuteronomy 6:4 declares, "The Lord is one," a confession often on the lips of God's people. But in the New Testament, Jesus receives this same title (Eph 1:2, 3, 15, 17; 3:11; 5:20; 6:23, 24). Thus, Paul's declaration of there being one Lord identifies Jesus with the God of the Old Testament. At the same time, Paul affirms that Jesus is the one Lord and affirms monotheism.

In fact, Paul's sevenfold affirmation of unity highlights the Trinity. He declares that there is "one Spirit ... one Lord ... one God and Father of all" (4:4–6). He links the Spirit with the one body (the church) because the presence of the Spirit is necessary for true unity to thrive. He links the Lord with the one faith the church professes and the one baptism it receives. And God the Father rules supremely over all his creation and, at the same time, is working in and through all things.

APPLY GOD'S WORD

Unity is essential to believers because it is central to the message we proclaim. The gospel is the good news that God has provided a way of reconciliation through the work of Jesus. Essentially the Christian message is news about how humanity can attain peace with God through his Son, Jesus Christ. When we neglect to display peace with each other, we compromise our message of peace. Jesus himself prayed, "The glory that you have given me I have given to them, that they may be one even as we are one, I in them and you in me, that they may become perfectly one, so that the world may know that you sent me and loved them even as you loved me" (John 17:22–23). The unity (or lack thereof) of believers impacts our testimony to the world. Unity (and the peace that comes from unity) is at the heart of our faith.

But unity cannot be attained by our own works or by our ideas. It must be established by the truths that are revealed in Scripture. Only a unity that is theologically grounded on the Triune God and his gospel will be sufficient to survive the attacks from without and the pressure from within. How is God leading you today to promote the unity of the one body of Christ?

PRAY

O God and Father, I acknowledge you as the source of all true unity. I confess that there is one body, one Spirit, one hope, one Lord, one faith, one baptism, and one God. Help me to promote unity in your church for the sake of the gospel and the sake of your name. Amen.

STUDY IT FURTHER

1. Paul uses the phrase "one body" as a reference to the church in Romans 12:4–5; 1 Corinthians 12:12–13, 20; and Colossians 3:15. Read each of these passages, noting differences and similarities to the Ephesians 4 passage.

2. The term "faith" can refer to the subjective act of belief (see Eph 1:15; 2:8; 3:12, 17; 6:16, 23) or the objective content of

that which is believed (see Rom 10:8; Gal 1:23; 3:23; Col 1:23; 2:7; 1 Tim 3:9; 4:1, 6). Read each of the passages mentioned above, distinguishing between the two different uses.

3. The phrase "God and Father" is found frequently in the New Testament (see Rom 15:6; 2 Cor 1:3; 11:31; Gal 1:4; Eph 1:3; Phil 4:20; 1 Thess 3:11, 13; 1 Pet 1:3; Rev 1:6). Why do you think this phrase is used so frequently?

Day 21

Ephesians 4:7–10

READ

But grace was given to each one of us
according to the measure of Christ's gift. Therefore it says,
"When he ascended on high he led a host of captives,
and he gave gifts to men."
(In saying, "He ascended," what does it mean
but that he had also descended into the lower regions,
the earth? He who descended is the one who also ascended
far above all the heavens, that he might fill all things.)

MEDITATE

Unity does not mean uniformity. Unity exists when people with different gifts work together to achieve the same goals. Uniformity is when people are forced to conform to a particular norm without taking into consideration their gifts or desires. Unity is biblical; uniformity is not. In Ephesians 4:1–6, Paul emphasizes the need for unity within the body of Christ, a unity founded on the truth that there is one Spirit, one Lord, and one God and Father of all. In the following verses (4:7–16), Paul stresses that such unity does not lead to uniformity since each individual is uniquely gifted, and it is the diversity of gifts that leads to the maturity of believers.

Christ has gifted every believer: Paul explains that Christ has sovereignly gifted every believer for the good of the church. He calls this gift grace because it is not something we earn or deserve, but it is something that every believer possesses ("grace was given to each one of us," 4:7). The purpose of this grace (gift) is that we might serve others and help the body of Christ to grow in maturity. This gift "was given," meaning that it doesn't originate with us but comes to us from Christ himself. And it is Christ who determines which gift is given and in what proportion ("according to the measure of Christ's gift," 4:7). It is not based on works or merit but is graciously and sovereignly given by the risen and reigning Lord.

Christ has ascended and earned the authority to gift every believer: In the following verse (4:8), Paul cites an Old Testament passage (Ps 68:18) to support the claim that Christ has sovereignly administered gifts to his people. In the context of Psalm 68, God the Divine Warrior defeats his enemies and ascends to his throne. Paul interprets this passage christologically so that Christ is the victorious conqueror who ascends to his heavenly throne after defeating the evil spiritual armies. Thus, having conquered his enemies, the triumphant Christ is able to distribute gifts to his followers.

In 4:9–10, Paul provides an inspired commentary on Psalm 68:18, highlighting the victory and ascension of Christ. In order for Christ to have ascended, he must have earlier descended, which is either a reference to Jesus's incarnation (and death) or to his descent to Hades and his defeat of the evil forces. But Paul's primary reason for mentioning Jesus's descent is to highlight his subsequent ascent. Not only did he ascend; he ascended "far above all the heavens" (4:10). That is, Christ has ascended to the place of highest honor and supremacy so "that he might fill all things" (4:10). Because Christ's lordship extends to the entire universe, he is able to gift his people sovereignly and uniquely. And he does this so that his diverse church will grow in maturity.

REFLECT ON CHRIST

Although the previous passage (4:1–6) highlighted the unity of the godhead (one Spirit, one Lord, one God and Father), this passage focuses solely on Christ and his sovereign administration of gifts to his people. First, it is Christ who gifts. When Paul uses the passive voice ("was given," 4:7), the implied subject is Christ. The following verses reiterate that Christ is the one who "gave gifts" (4:8) to his people and that "he gave" (4:11) various types of leaders to the church. Second, Christ gives gifts to all. Nobody is left out since grace is given "to each one" (4:7). Third, Christ gifts all differently. He gives gifts in different measures. Not everybody receives the same gift, and not everybody is equally gifted. Gifts are not earned or deserved, and Christ gives as he sees best for the maturation of his church. Finally, Christ has earned the right to gift. He descended, taking on human flesh and serving humanity by dying on the cross. He defeated death and the devil through his resurrection and ascension. Therefore, he has earned the right and authority to distribute gifts according to his divine purpose.

APPLY GOD'S WORD

Do you think of yourself as "gifted"? According to Paul, all believers are gifted. That is, all believers have been graced with spiritual gifts by the resurrected and ascended Christ. What are your gifts? Have you identified them? Have others confirmed them? Are you exercising them for the good of the church? Are you honing them and developing them so that you are a more effective servant of Christ? Do you envy the gifts of others? Or do you celebrate the diversity of gifts and giftings in the body? Do you boast or feel a sense of superiority because your gifts are often viewed as more significant than the gifts of others? Peter exhorts us, "Humble yourselves, therefore, under the mighty hand of God so that at the proper time he may exalt you" (1 Pet 5:6). Because these are gifts, there is no room for pride. Rather, let us use our gifts for the expansion of God's kingdom. He is the giver of every good and perfect gift (Jas 1:17), and the one who gives gets the glory.

PRAY

Christ, you humbled yourself and became a servant
for the sake of others. Help me to do the same.
You obeyed the will of your Father for the sake of others.
Help me to do the same.
And you used your gifts to expand the kingdom
of God. Help me to do the same. Amen.

STUDY IT FURTHER

1. In Ephesians 4:7, Paul notes that grace has been given "to each one of us." How do 1 Corinthians 12:7 and 1 Peter 4:10 describe that which has been given to each person?

2. Read Romans 12:4–8 and 1 Corinthians 12:4–11. Although these lists do not represent all the gifts, which of these gifts do you think you possess?

3. Although there is debate regarding the location of Christ's descent "into the lower regions" (4:9), the reason for discussing the descent is to highlight Christ's ascent. How does Ephesians 1:20–21 relate to this passage, specifically his ascension?

Day 22

Ephesians 4:11–12

READ

And he gave the apostles, the prophets, the evangelists,
the shepherds and teachers, to equip the saints
for the work of ministry, for building up the body of Christ …

MEDITATE

In the previous passage, Paul declared that the victorious and sovereign Christ has graciously gifted every believer. Today's passage focuses on gifts given to leaders. Christ does not merely bless the church with spiritual gifts; he gives actual leaders who are needed for the unity and maturity of the church.

Christ has given leaders to the church: Paul includes five types of leaders who are gifted by Christ and given to the church: apostles, prophets, evangelists, shepherds, and teachers. First, Christ has given apostles. Paul labels himself as an apostle (1:1), and he says apostles and prophets provide the foundation for the church (2:20). This latter statement could be taken to mean (1) that the apostolic witness is now inscribed as Scripture, which has become the foundation for the church (and thus there are no more apostles like the Twelve and Paul, who wrote inspired Scripture), or (2) that Paul is referring to the apostolic gift found in missionaries and church planters (and thus the gift continues today). Second, Christ has given prophets. This is probably not a reference to Old Testament prophets but those early Christians who spoke God's truth to the church. Third, Christ has given evangelists. Because this term is used only two other times in the New Testament (Acts 21:8 and 2 Tim 4:5), it is difficult to know their precise role. But as their name conveys, they were those who often traveled to preach the good news (inside and outside the church). Finally, Christ gave shepherds (or pastors) and teachers. Because of the construction found in the original language, these are best seen not as two distinct groups but as overlapping (with shepherds being a subset of teachers). That is, all shepherds teach but not all teachers shepherd (pastor).

Christ has given leaders to equip the church: Paul does not stop after listing the leaders who are gifted to the church. He then provides two reasons for such leaders. First, they are given "to equip the saints for the work of ministry" (4:12). In other words, Christ gives leaders who equip the congregation (the saints) to do the work of the ministry. The leaders aren't simply paid to do the work of the ministry. Their task is to equip the congregation for such work. After all, gifts have been given to every believer (4:7). This verse has huge implications for how we view church leaders, especially church staff. The ministry is not only given to a select few who are drawing a salary from the church. Instead, leaders are given the task of equipping the congregation to do the work of ministry.

Christ has given leaders to build up the church: The second reason Christ gifts leaders to the church is "for building up the body of Christ" (4:12). The church is built up (i.e., spiritually strengthened) when leaders faithfully train the congregation to use their gifts in the church. Paul is probably speaking qualitatively (strengthening the existing body) and not quantitatively (adding members to the body), though both are important. The goal is that the body of Christ becomes spiritually mature.

REFLECT ON CHRIST

Jesus himself said, "It is more blessed to give than to receive" (Acts 20:35). These were not mere words for Jesus; they reflect his life and actions. He healed the sick, welcomed the outcast, and proclaimed the good news of the kingdom. He gave his time and his energy to others, especially to his disciples. He taught them and trained them and sent them out so that they could continue to announce the arrival of the kingdom of God. He then gave his life on behalf of others—others who are described in Scripture as powerless, ungodly, sinners, and enemies (Rom 5:6–10).

In our passage today, we see that Jesus continues to give. Jesus is the one who blesses the church with leaders, and the purpose of such leaders is to build up the body of Christ. The church belongs to Christ. He loved it, purchased it, and blesses it so that it grows in maturity. "All things were created through him and for him" (Col 1:16).

APPLY GOD'S WORD

All believers are gifted, but some are gifted to serve as leaders. Gifts alone, however, are never enough to qualify someone for leadership. Those who serve as leaders should also have a desire to serve (1 Tim 3:1) and the commensurate godly character (1 Tim 3:1–13; Titus 1:5–9; 1 Pet 5:1–3). Many leadership positions (including the apostles, prophets, evangelists, and pastor-teachers) include a teaching component because the ministry of speaking or teaching God's word is crucial for the unity and maturity of the church (1 Tim 3:2; Titus 1:9).

The task of church leaders is not to do the work of the ministry but to equip the congregation for such work. All believers are called to serve God since all are called as priests (1 Pet 2:9). Do you view yourself as gifted by Christ? Do you view yourself as a priest of God? Do you use your gifts to build up the body of Christ? Or do you view paid leaders as the professionals who should do the work since they receive a salary from the church? According to Paul, the leaders are given to equip the congregation to effectively carry out the work of the ministry.

PRAY

Christ, thank you for giving leaders to the church.
Bless them and strengthen them and help them
to effectively equip every member to contribute
to the growth of your church. Help me to faithfully
and joyfully serve where there is a need. Amen.

STUDY IT FURTHER

1. Read the following passages regarding New Testament prophets, and record insights as to their function in the early church: Acts 11:27–28; 13:1; 15:32; 21:10–11; and 1 Corinthians 14:24–25. Do you think there are prophets today?

2. The term "evangelist" is only used two other times in the New Testament, with Philip (Acts 21:8) and Timothy (2 Tim 4:5). Is there evidence that those who were called this term were involved in a traveling ministry (see Acts 8:4–5, 35, 40; 2 Tim 4:9, 21)? What does this mean for modern-day evangelism?

3. The KJV places a comma after each phrase in Ephesians 4:12, so that there are three (instead of two) purposes of Christ giving leaders to the church ("for the perfecting of the saints, for the work of the ministry, for the edifying of the body of Christ"). How does this change the meaning of the text?

Day 23

Ephesians 4:13–16

READ

... until we all attain to the unity of the faith
and of the knowledge of the Son of God, to mature manhood,
to the measure of the stature of the fullness of Christ,
so that we may no longer be children, tossed to and fro
by the waves and carried about by every wind of doctrine,
by human cunning, by craftiness in deceitful schemes.
Rather, speaking the truth in love, we are to grow up
in every way into him who is the head,
into Christ, from whom the whole body, joined
and held together by every joint with which
it is equipped, when each part is working properly,
makes the body grow so that it builds itself up in love.

MEDITATE

Christ has given leaders to the church in order to equip the members of Christ's body for works of service. But why is it important for members to serve the church and do the work of the ministry? In this passage, Paul explains the goal is the unity and maturity of the church.

Unity is built around the faith: Unity for the sake of unity will not endure. Unity must have a centripetal force pulling it together. Paul mentions that our unity is built around "the faith" and "the knowledge of the Son of God" (4:13). In this context, faith does not refer to one's personal commitment but to the objective truth and doctrines of Christianity. Thus, believers should have a firm commitment to the historical teachings of the Bible that have been "once for all delivered to the saints" (Jude 3). More specifically, we rally around those essential truths related to Jesus, God's Son. Our unity must be founded on the person and work of Jesus.

Maturity is conforming to the image of Christ: What does godly maturity look like? Paul exhorts us to attain to "mature manhood to the measure of the stature of the fullness of Christ" (4:13). Maturity looks like Jesus. It is seeking to pray like him, respond like him, love like him, and serve sacrificially like him. Christ provides the standard that we seek to emulate.

Those who are mature are no longer children. Although sometimes in Scripture children can be a model for believers, here they represent those who do not have a firm grasp on the truth. Children can be gullible, easily tricked, and deceived. Children, in this case, are those who are spiritually immature, not sure about what to believe, who to trust, or how to live. They are "tossed to and fro by the waves and carried about" (4:14). They don't know which direction to go and are easily pushed into various false teachings. Consequently, we are exhorted to be firmly grounded in the apostolic teaching so that we may grow into mature followers of Christ.

Rather than being immature and unstable, we are to speak the truth of the gospel (4:15). But sometimes we can become so truth focused that we forget to model the compassion and love of Christ. So Paul adds that we must speak not with callousness or cold-heartedness but "in love" (4:15). Our goal is to become more like our Savior. As the head of the church, he nourishes and supplies all that the body needs for its growth. All believers are joined together in this body, and all believers are equipped to serve. Each person must do their part for the body to function properly. Christ has gifted and empowered each one of us so that we can use our gifts for the benefit of others and for the building up of his church.

REFLECT ON CHRIST

In a way, this passage could seem human-centered: *We* need to attain unity; *we* need to achieve maturity; *we* should no longer be like immature children who are easily swayed and deceived; *we* should speak the truth in love; *we* are to grow up in every way; *we* must each participate in serving the body. But such a reading misses the bigger picture and the Christ-centered focus of this text.

First, Christ is the heart of our faith. Paul urges us to seek the unity of the faith, a faith that is centered on "the knowledge of the Son of God" (4:13). The very title of our faith, "Christianity," reveals that Jesus is not simply one part of what we believe. He embodies the fulfillment of all the promises of God. Second, Christ is the model for our faith. Elsewhere Paul states, "Imitate me, as I also imitate Christ" (1 Cor 11:1 CSB). Jesus's attitudes and actions are the template we follow to maturity. Third, Christ is the head of the church. He is not only our model; he is our Lord. He purchased the church with his blood and reigns over it. Fourth, Christ equips the church. He has gifted each member and equips us for service.

APPLY GOD'S WORD

Do you consider yourself mature in the faith? Have you seen spiritual growth in your life over the past few years? Spiritual growth is usually a slow process that occurs over months and years, but it is also something that does not occur in isolation. When Paul speaks of growth, he is not thinking of personal, individual growth but of the maturity of the body of Christ. Notice that he uses the terms "we" and "body" several times. He is thinking collectively. Furthermore, this body that is joined and held together also grows together. Paul's concept of maturity is one that involves the entire body, not just individual parts. We grow when we work in unity for a common purpose as we serve our Lord and Savior.

Maturity is not only about *doing*; it is also about *being*. In other words, thinking and meditating on Christ (being) is often the key to serving (doing). With such a Christ-centered passage, we would be amiss if we didn't stop to thank God for his plan to unite all things in Christ. He is our Lord, our Savior, our provider, our sustainer, our model, and our friend.

PRAY

God, help me to seek the unity of your church.
Help me to become mature, to become more like Christ
and to faithfully serve your church. I know that I cannot
do this on my own, so I ask for your strength. Thank you
for Christ who is my Lord, Savior, and example. Amen.

STUDY IT FURTHER

1. Read back through Ephesians, paying attention to the uses of "we" and other terms that emphasize the corporate nature of the faith. How has being part of the body of Christ grown your faith?

2. Read Hebrews 5:12–6:1 and note how this passage speaks to the need to become mature followers of Christ. Can you identify an area in your life that you need to mature in? What is one step you could take to move toward greater maturity?

3. Spiritual maturity is often metaphorically related to physical maturity. In other words, behaving like a child means being immature whereas behaving like an adult means being mature. Read Matthew 19:14 and 1 Peter 2:2–3, and note the positive side of being like a child. Is there a childlike trait that you need to grow in?

Day 24

Ephesians 4:17–19

READ

Now this I say and testify in the Lord, that you must no longer walk as the Gentiles do, in the futility of their minds. They are darkened in their understanding, alienated from the life of God because of the ignorance that is in them, due to their hardness of heart. They have become callous and have given themselves up to sensuality, greedy to practice every kind of impurity.

MEDITATE

Being a Christian doesn't mean you affirm Jesus as your Lord and Savior and now, with your sins forgiven and with a ticket to heaven, you can live however you please. Rather, the New Testament writers consistently emphasize the need for Christians to live differently. We are not to live as the gentiles do (4:17). The gentiles were known for their lifestyle of drunkenness and immorality. But, as we will see, their lifestyle isn't the only problem; it begins with their minds and hearts. They act a certain way because they are a certain type of person with a certain type of mindset. Christians, however, have a renewed mind and a renewed heart and therefore are expected to live differently.

Don't live as unbelievers who have corrupt minds: Paul begins chapter 4 with a call to live a certain way: "I … urge you to walk in a manner worthy of the calling to which you have been called" (4:1). He now resumes this focus by calling his readers to abandon the ungodly lifestyle that they embraced (or approved of) before they were converted. But before Paul speaks to the actions of the gentiles, he highlights their corrupt minds. First, unconverted gentiles walk "in the futility of their minds" (4:17). Their actions followed their corrupt minds. Second, they are described as those "darkened in their understanding" (4:18). Unregenerate gentiles do not see things through God's perspective, because their understanding is darkened and corrupted. Third, they are full of "ignorance" because of "their hardness of heart" (4:18). Their hearts are obstinate, unable to convict them of sin. Finally, Paul says they "have become callous" (4:19). Because they have lost the capacity to feel embarrassment or shame, they plunge themselves into sin without thinking twice. With such futile minds, darkened understanding, and callous hearts, there is no pulling back from sin.

Don't live as unbelievers who have impure actions: Jesus said that from the overflow of the heart, the mouth speaks (Luke 6:45). Our actions follow our heart. If our heart has become calloused, then impure actions are sure to follow. Because unconverted gentiles had become dead of feeling, they gave "themselves up to sensuality, greedy to practice every kind of impurity" (4:19). Those without the Spirit freely give themselves to sexual sins and all other types of impure living, and they are not satisfied but "greedy to practice" such behavior. Paul urges us to avoid this kind of lifestyle since it is characteristic of those separated from God.

Don't live as unbelievers who are alienated from God: Those who live like unbelieving gentiles demonstrate that they are "alienated from the life of God" (4:18). Note that such a lifestyle does not cause one to be alienated but rather is the result of being estranged from God, the source of life and power to overcome sin and temptation. Paul earlier reminded his gentile readers that they were "alienated from the commonwealth of Israel" (2:12) but now, by blood of Christ, they have been brought near to God (2:13). Apart from the life-giving power of God, we will remain dead in our sins (2:1, 5).

REFLECT ON CHRIST

Paul begins this passage with a note of solemnity: "Now this I say and testify in the Lord" (4:17). The seriousness of Paul's appeal is brought out in two ways—by the verb "testify" and the phrase "in the Lord." Earlier Paul notes that he is "a prisoner for the Lord" (4:1), and here he emphasizes that the source of his authority comes from the Lord Jesus. His message is one of grave condemnation for those apart from Christ. It is a stark reminder of what life is like when we are separated from Christ, alienated from God's covenant people, and without hope. Although Christ is not mentioned again in this passage, we can be grateful for the hope we have attained by our new life in Christ, which has transformed us from a life of darkness to one of light.

APPLY GOD'S WORD

The way we think affects the way we live. If we think that we will not be held accountable for our actions, if there is no life after death, if there is no judgment at the end of time, then we will live accordingly. Paul emphasizes that the lifestyle of unregenerate gentiles is the result of their corrupt mindset. Degenerate thinking naturally leads to impure actions. Consequently, they are given to sensuality, greed, and impurity (4:19).

It can be difficult to live differently than those around us. Paul's readers were gentile Christians living in a predominantly gentile context. He urges them to "no longer walk as the Gentiles do" (4:17). He expected them to abandon the sinful lifestyle that they once embraced. Why was Paul compelled to exhort them in his letter? As gentile Christians, their lives should look transformed by the power of the Spirit within them. They were no longer slaves to sin but slaves to Christ. In this way, their ordinary lives were extraordinary examples of Christ's power and grace to the people around them. We must be mindful of living separate from the world—to be *in* the world but not *of* the world—as witnesses for Christ.

PRAY

God, apart from you I can do nothing.
I know that on my own I will fall and I will fail.
But you have called me to live differently from those who actively rebel against you and your word. So, please work in me and through me so I am able to put away sin and to put on the new life that is found in Christ. Amen.

STUDY IT FURTHER

1. The word "futility" (4:17) is sometimes translated "meaningless" or "vanity." See Ecclesiastes, where it is used to describe life apart from the fear of God (e.g., 1:2, 14; 2:1, 11, 15, 17, 19).

2. Paul says that unbelieving gentiles are estranged from God "because of the ignorance that is in them" (4:18). But if such

people are ignorant, does that mean they are not culpable before God? See Romans 1:19–21 and 1 Thessalonians 4:5.

3. The reflexive pronoun "themselves" (4:19) indicates that it was the gentiles' own initiative that led them into immorality. How does that relate to God giving over people to their sins (see Rom 1:24–28)?

Day 25

Ephesians 4:20–24

READ

But that is not the way you learned Christ!—assuming that you have heard about him and were taught in him, as the truth is in Jesus, to put off your old self, which belongs to your former manner of life and is corrupt through deceitful desires, and to be renewed in the spirit of your minds, and to put on the new self, created after the likeness of God in true righteousness and holiness.

MEDITATE

The pull of temptation and sin is strong, and fighting against it requires a renewed mind and renewed desires. After urging the Ephesians not to live as unbelievers, Paul reminds his readers that the apostolic message they received included the admonition to live godly lives. Such living involves both putting off and putting on. We are to flee sin, and we are to embrace the truth and pursue godliness.

We must put off the old self: In verse 22, Paul says "to put off your old self, which belongs to your former manner of life and is corrupt through deceitful desires." Just as old, dirty clothes are taken off and laid aside, we are to put aside our previous lifestyle with its luring lusts and passions. The phrase "old self" refers to our former, unregenerate nature that still lingers within us. This corrupted old self includes the sinful passions that characterize unbelievers and that ultimately lead to their ruin. Because these desires are opposed to God and the gospel, Paul reminds us not to be ruled by them but to be actively engaged in putting them aside.

We must be renewed in our minds: In addition to putting off sin, we need to have our minds renewed (4:23). Such renewal is not something we do to ourselves but something God works in us. And yet, we are exhorted to have our minds renewed since we have the responsibility to put ourselves in a situation where God's Spirit-empowered renewal will be achieved. We must yield ourselves to God, who works through his Spirit to renew our inner person. As Paul similarly writes in Romans 12:2: "Do not be conformed to this world, but be transformed by the renewal of your mind."

We must put on the new self: It is not enough to put off or flee sin. In place of a sinful nature, we must "put on the new self" (4:24). That is, we must seek that which is good and pure. Similar to the verb "put off," the verb "put on" is typically used in regard to clothing. Here it is used figuratively for taking on characteristics or virtues of something. Paul urges us to actively pursue a lifestyle consistent with our new nature. This new self is "created after the likeness of God" (4:24), indicating that God is both the one who creates (the author of life) and that he creates according to his own image (the pattern of life). Elsewhere, Paul states, "[You] have put on the new self, which is being renewed in knowledge after the image of its creator" (Col 3:10). The new self is also created "in true righteousness and holiness" (4:24), both of which are characteristics of God. Paul instructs us to take off and flee from a lifestyle that is contrary to the gospel of Jesus Christ and to put on and pursue becoming more like God himself—a life marked by righteousness and holiness.

REFLECT ON CHRIST

This passage begins with a christological emphasis: "But that is not the way you learned Christ!—assuming that you have heard about him and were taught in him, as the truth is in Jesus" (4:20–21). The phrase "you learned Christ" is a bit unusual. Often we speak of learning about content (teaching, doctrine, etc.) or behavior (love, honor, etc.), but here, Paul speaks of learning a person. Perhaps the closest parallel passage is found in Colossians 2:6–7: "Therefore, as you received Christ Jesus the Lord, so walk in him, rooted and built up in him and established in the faith, just as you were taught." But how is it that we are to learn Christ? Andrew Lincoln notes, "Since Christians believed that Christ was a living person whose presence was mediated by the proclamation and teaching about him, learning Christ involved not only learning about, but also being shaped by, the risen Christ who was the source of a new way of life as well as of a new relationship with God."[3] Christ is both the content of apostolic teaching and the model of how we are to live.

APPLY GOD'S WORD

The Christian life often consists of paradoxes. We have died to sin (Rom 6:2), and yet we are instructed not to let sin reign in our bodies (Rom 6:12). Both seemingly contradictory realities are true. We died to sin through our union with Christ, but because our old nature, though dead, still haunts us, we must continually fight not to let it rule over our lives. Similarly, we

3. Andrew Lincoln, *Ephesians*, Word Biblical Commentary (Word, 1990), 280.

have been given a new self in Christ, yet we must actively take off the old self and put on the new self. Affirming the reality of being a new creation in Christ (see 2 Cor 5:17) does not mean we can neglect the need to fight to become what we already are. We are given a new nature that is created according to God's own nature of righteousness and holiness (4:24). In one sense, we already are the new self. And yet, as our old self haunts us, Paul urges us to continually put on the new self.

This is not a contradiction but reflects two important truths: (1) in Christ we are made new, and (2) we have not yet fully become what we will be. Consequently, we must continually seek to put off the old and put on the new. What is God calling you today to put off? What is he asking you to put on?

PRAY

God, help me to be like Christ since he embodies the truth. Help me to put off the old self and the lifestyle that is contrary to the gospel, and help me to put on the new self that is according to righteousness and holiness. Amen.

STUDY IT FURTHER

1. The concept of taking off (or casting off or putting away) is found elsewhere in Paul. Read Romans 13:12 and Colossians 3:8, and note what believers are to put aside.

2. Read 2 Corinthians 3:18 and Titus 3:5, paying attention to the role of the Holy Spirit in the life of the believer. How has the Spirit renewed your mind?

3. The concept of putting on is seen in Romans 13:12, 14; Galatians 3:27; Ephesians 6:11, 14; Colossians 3:10; and 1 Thessalonians 5:8. What specifically are we to "put on" in each of these passages?

Day 26

Ephesians 4:25–32

READ

Therefore, having put away falsehood, let each one of you speak the truth with his neighbor, for we are members one of another. Be angry and do not sin; do not let the sun go down on your anger, and give no opportunity to the devil. Let the thief no longer steal, but rather let him labor, doing honest work with his own hands, so that he may have something to share with anyone in need. Let no corrupting talk come out of your mouths, but only such as is good for building up, as fits the occasion, that it may give grace to those who hear. And do not grieve the Holy Spirit of God, by whom you were sealed for the day of redemption. Let all bitterness and wrath and anger and clamor and slander be put away from you, along with all malice. Be kind to one another, tenderhearted, forgiving one another, as God in Christ forgave you.

MEDITATE

Like children, adults don't like being told what to do. We are independent-minded, able to provide for ourselves, and we make our own decisions. Receiving instruction can be difficult for us. But in some circumstances, we seek out guidance. When I changed the A/C blower motor in my car, I searched for a video that would give me step-by-step instructions because I lacked the knowledge to make the change I needed. In this text, Paul provides practical instructions for what it means to put off the old self and put on the new self. These commands are not meant to confine us but to liberate us, so that we will have the freedom to walk according to our calling (4:1). In these eight verses, Paul offers about a dozen prohibitions (what *not* to do) and commands (what to do). In particular, these exhortations relate to the personal relationships within the church, especially those that promote unity among the people of God.

Actions to avoid: Paul's earlier instruction to "put off" (4:22) does not remain a vague or abstract idea. In this passage, the apostle unpacks what such action looks like on a daily basis. First, he states that we should "put away falsehood" (4:25; see Col 3:9). God's people must not lie to one another (which includes not telling half-truths). Second, when we have righteous anger, we are not to sin, giving opportunity to the devil (4:26–27). This command reminds us that it is easy to go from "righteous anger" to "sinful anger" (see Jas 1:19–20). Anger in and of itself is not necessarily bad, but anger expressed out of envy, pride, or other sinful motives is ungodly behavior. And when we cross the line into sinful anger, we should deal with such sin immediately so that it does not fester, giving opportunity for the devil to exploit our sin. Third, we are not to steal (4:28), an action that is forbidden in both the Old Testament and the New Testament. Taking things that do not belong to us (including stealing time from our employers) is a temptation that we must avoid. Fourth, we must "let no corrupting talk come out of" our mouths (4:29). Once again, Paul emphasizes the importance of our speech. The term "corrupt" refers to that which is "spoiled," "rotten," or "putrid." Here, it signifies that which is harmful and tears down and does not build up. Fifth, we are warned not to "grieve the Holy Spirit" (4:30). Based on the context, the Holy Spirit is especially grieved when followers of Christ speak unkindly to each other. Finally, we are to put away all bitterness, wrath, anger, clamor, slander, and malice (4:31). There may be an intentional progression of sins in these verses from an inner disposition of bitterness to an outward display of harmful speech. All of these sins must be put away because they are contrary to the work of the Spirit of God.

Actions to embrace: Paul also calls us to put on or embrace godly virtues. First, we are to "speak the truth" (4:25). Instead of speaking falsehoods, believers must speak the truth to each other. Second, we should have appropriate anger on certain occasions. Not all anger is sinful, since Jesus demonstrated anger (see Mark 3:5). And yet we must be careful not to cross the line (see 4:31). Third, Paul instructs us to work hard "doing honest work with [our] own hands" (4:28). The motivation of such work is so that we "may have something to share with anyone in need" (4:28), a characteristic of the early church. Not stealing is good, but sharing what we have is the way of Christ. Fourth, our words should not corrupt but should positively build up (4:29). Our speech should be beneficial and wholesome, so "that it may give grace to those who hear" (4:29). Finally, we should be kind, tenderhearted, and forgiving to others (4:32; see Col 3:12–13; 1 Pet 3:8). Christians are expected to model the life and behavior of Jesus, our Savior.

REFLECT ON CHRIST

The final exhortation puts all of the previous prohibitions and commands in perspective. We are to forgive one another "as God in Christ Jesus forgave you" (4:32). In Colossians, Paul states, "As the Lord has forgiven you, so you also must forgive" (Col 3:13). Because we have freely received grace from God through the sacrificial work of Christ, we are called to graciously forgive others who have wronged us. We have wronged and offended God by our rebellion and sin, but God made us alive and restored us to fellowship with him. Having received such forgiveness, we should be the first to offer forgiveness to others.

APPLY GOD'S WORD

This passage is full of things to do and things not to do. It may even seem overwhelming. None of us is perfect, and we all struggle in our fight against sin and in our embrace of righteousness. But throughout this passage, we also see truths to motivate us to right living. We are members of one another (4:25), sealed with the Holy Spirit (4:30), and forgiven (4:32). As a beloved child of God (see 5:1) who is indwelt and sealed with God's Spirit and forgiven, what is one area of putting off and putting on that which God would have you focus on today?

PRAY

Oh Lord, you have sought me, rescued me,
forgiven me, and empowered me. With your strength,
help me to live gladly according to your word.
May your word be to me more valuable than gold
and sweeter than honey—for the sake of your holy name.
Amen.

STUDY IT FURTHER

1. Believers are encouraged to share with those in need (4:28). Helping each other was a characteristic of the early believers. Read Acts 20:35; 1 Timothy 5:8; Titus 3:14; James 1:27; and 1 John 3:17, and take note of the expectation that Christians will help others in need. Is there someone in your life that you might be able to help?

2. The term "corrupt" (*sapros*) refers to something which is spoiled, rotten, or putrid. Study the following passages in Matthew to see how this term is used to describe trees (Matt 7:17–18), fruit (Matt 7:17–18), and fish (Matt 13:48).

3. We love because God first loved us (1 John 4:19). And we forgive because God first forgave us. Read Psalm 25:7; 31:19; and 65:11, where kindness (goodness) is an attribute of God that is displayed toward his people. Pray for a deep sense of God's love.

Day 27

Ephesians 5:1–2

READ

*Therefore be imitators of God, as beloved children.
And walk in love, as Christ loved us and gave himself
up for us, a fragrant offering and sacrifice to God.*

MEDITATE

In this passage, Paul gives us two more commands: imitate God, and walk in love.

Imitate God: The well-known saying "imitation is the sincerest form of flattery" conveys the idea that copying or mimicking someone pays tribute to them since they are deemed worthy of the effort it takes to follow in their steps. If such is true of humanity, how much more is it true of God? In this passage, Paul calls us to "be imitators of God" (5:1). But how do we imitate someone who is unseen? By using the word "therefore," Paul signals that this passage is closely related to the previous passage (4:25–32), especially verse 32: "Be kind to one another, tenderhearted, forgiving one another, as God in Christ forgave you." In this context, imitating God means forgiving one another. The forgiveness that we received from God occurred while we were his enemies. We violated his commands, rebelling against the king of the universe. Instead of worshiping God, we worshiped the creation. And yet, God forgave us because of the work of Christ. Imitating God means being willing to forgive others, even others who have wronged and offended us. We are called to make God's activity the pattern of our lives.

But Paul doesn't offer us a raw command. The injunction comes with an amazing truth—we are God's "beloved children" (5:1). Here, Paul provides the basis on which we are to imitate God. He is our Father, and we are the children he loves. This theme of being adopted into God's family goes back to Ephesians 1:5, "[In love] he predestined us for adoption to himself as sons through Jesus Christ, according to the purpose of his will." Because we have been adopted into God's family, we should pattern our lifestyle according to the head of the house. As God's children who are dearly loved, we should want to be like our loving Father. This relationship both requires *and enables* us to imitate our heavenly Father.

Walk in love: This second command is not distinct from the first but is an example of what it means to imitate God. We also imitate God by loving others. We are to be characterized as those who have a genuine love for each other. Once again, Paul doesn't offer this admonition in isolation but provides a comparison: we should love others as Christ loves us (5:2), which fuels our motivation (we should love *because* Christ loves us). How does Christ love us? Paul adds that he "gave himself up for us, a fragrant offering and sacrifice to God" (5:2). Not only did the Father give his only Son, but the Son freely surrendered his life. And he gave himself for our benefit and in our place as an offering and sacrifice—a sacrifice that was accepted by the Father because it was a fragrant, or well-pleasing, sacrifice.

We are to imitate God by walking in love, the type of sacrificial love we see demonstrated by Jesus on the cross.

REFLECT ON CHRIST

Christ is the focus of our forgiveness, and he is the focus of our love. We should forgive others because God in Christ forgave us (4:32), and we should love others "as Christ loved us and gave himself up for us" (5:2). God's love is eminently displayed in his Son who freely surrendered his life. Jesus declares, "The good shepherd lays down his life for the sheep. … No one takes it from me, but I lay it down of my own accord. I have authority to lay it down, and I have authority to take it up again" (John 10:11, 18). He later adds, "Greater love has no one than this, that someone lay down his life for his friends" (John 15:13).

The pronoun "himself" in verse 2 further signifies that Jesus took the initiative to offer his life as a sacrifice in the place of others (see 5:25). He willingly offered himself to pay the penalty of our sins. He became a curse so that we might receive the blessings promised to Abraham (Gal 3:13–14). Thus, all the Old Testament offerings and sacrifices are now fulfilled in Christ, who once and for all made atonement for sins.

APPLY GOD'S WORD

Jesus tells us that loving God and loving neighbor are the two greatest commands (Matt 22:37–39). Paul indicates that love is greater than faith and hope (1 Cor 13:13). Of all the commands that Paul offers in 4:25–5:2, the exhortation to love stands supreme. The way we imitate God is to love as he loves, and the way that he loves is seen most clearly in the way in which Jesus freely sacrificed himself in the place of sinners.

Why is love so important? Why is love the highest virtue? It is because when we love others, it necessarily means that we embrace other virtues. When we love others, we will not lie to each other, yell at each other, or be bitter and angry toward each other. Instead, we will speak the truth, build up one another, and be kind and forgiving. As you ponder your actions to others, are they characterized by hate or by love? Today, focus on loving others as Christ loves you. The right actions will follow a heart focused on Christ.

PRAY

Oh Lord, as your beloved child, help me to walk in love toward others—others that I like and even others that are difficult to like. Help me to remember the sacrifice of Christ who willingly gave up his life for me. May his sacrifice motivate me to love others. Amen.

STUDY IT FURTHER

1. This is the only text where Paul exhorts his readers to imitate God (but see Matt 5:44; Luke 6:35–36). Read the following texts and note what believers are exhorted to imitate (1 Cor 4:16; 11:1; Phil 3:17; 1 Thess 1:6; 2:14; 2 Thess 3:7, 9). Would you be confident to exhort others to imitate you?

2. We can imitate God since we are his beloved children. Read Ephesians 1:4–5; 2:4–7; 5:25–27 to recall how God's love is displayed to us.

3. The substitutionary atonement of Jesus (i.e., that Jesus died in the place of others) is a central tenet in the Christian faith. See the following passages that highlight this important theme: Eph 5:25; 2 Cor 5:14, 21; Gal 1:4; 3:13; 1 Tim 2:6; Titus 2:14. What does Jesus's atonement reveal about his love for us?

Day 28

Ephesians 5:3–6

READ

But sexual immorality and all impurity or covetousness must not even be named among you, as is proper among saints. Let there be no filthiness nor foolish talk nor crude joking, which are out of place, but instead let there be thanksgiving. For you may be sure of this, that everyone who is sexually immoral or impure, or who is covetous (that is, an idolater), has no inheritance in the kingdom of Christ and God. Let no one deceive you with empty words, for because of these things the wrath of God comes upon the sons of disobedience.

MEDITATE

After encouraging us to imitate God by walking in love, Paul now offers several sins to avoid. The Bible is not primarily a book about morals. It is a book about how the Creator redeems fallen humanity through the sacrifice of his Son. But the Bible does contain morals, and there are certain expectations as to how Christians are to live. We are not free to decide our own morality or follow the longings of our sin-prone hearts. We are called to walk worthy of our calling, which includes avoiding certain blatant sins that should not be associated with a believer.

The first triad of sins given comprises sexual immorality (*porneia*), impurity, and covetousness (5:3). In the following verse, Paul offers another triad of vices that believers must avoid: filthiness, foolish talk, and crude joking (5:4). These are sins of speech that also carry sexual connotations. For example, "filthiness" means "to act in defiance of social and moral standards, with resulting disgrace, embarrassment, and shame."[4] The third triad mirrors the first as the apostle again references the sexually immoral, impure, and covetous (5:5). Paul also supplies three reasons why Christians must abstain from these sins.

Such sins are not fitting for a believer: He states that these sins "must not even be named among you, as is proper among saints" (5:3). These sins should be universally rejected and absent from believers' lives so that no one would associate this sinful behavior with the followers of Christ. Christians are called to live holy and blameless lives before God (1:4). Our behavior should be consistent with our identity as God's chosen people.

Such sins signify that a person is not a child of God: Paul says such people have "no inheritance in the kingdom of Christ and God" (5:5). The concept of inheritance includes familial connections. Those who fail to avoid the vices mentioned above have no inheritance because they are not imitating their Father, demonstrating that they are not legitimate children. The meaning is not that anyone who commits the sins of sexual immorality, impurity, or covetousness is excluded from God's heavenly

---

4. Johannes P. Louw, and Eugene A. Nida, *Greek-English Lexicon of the New Testament Based on Semantic Domains*, 2 vols. (United Bible Societies, 1988), §88.149.

kingdom. Rather, the meaning is anyone whose life is *characterized* by these sins will not enter God's kingdom.

Such sins expose one to the wrath of God: Apparently, some in the church, who refused to take sin seriously, were attempting to coerce others in the congregation to follow ungodly passions. Paul solemnly warns that those whose actions are characterized by sinful practices will experience God's fierce judgment (5:6). True believers will not face God's wrath because they are sealed and filled with God's Spirit and are no longer "children of wrath" (2:3). Instead, they have a sure inheritance (1:13–14). God's wrath is reserved for those who have spurned his Son, who are devoid of the Spirit, and consequently who live as unregenerate gentiles who "have given themselves to sensuality, greedy to practice every kind of impurity" (4:19). Such sins are not consistent with the way of Christ and must be avoided.

REFLECT ON CHRIST

Paul writes that instead of filthiness, foolish talk, and crude joking, "Let there be thanksgiving" (5:4). In response to the salvation that God offers us (choosing us, redeeming us, providing us an inheritance, sealing us with his Spirit, etc.), we should not seek to indulge the flesh but should thank God for his grace. Indeed, God is the source of "every good gift and every perfect gift" (Jas 1:17). And when we offer thanks to God for our redemption, we can't help but thank him for Christ. Because of our union with him, we have been made alive, raised, and seated with him in the heavenly places (Eph 2:5–6). All the blessings that we experience as believers are because we have been united to Christ (1:3).

Interestingly, Paul references the kingdom not as "the kingdom of God" but as "the kingdom of Christ and God" (5:5), a unique expression in the New Testament. The apostle is emphasizing the reign and rule of Christ, who is even now ruling with the Father over all his creation (see 1:20–23). Jesus is the King over all other kings and the Lord over all other lords.

APPLY GOD'S WORD

Paul's list of sins covers three broad categories: sexual immorality, greed, and inappropriate language. Because these vices were common in first-century Greco-Roman culture, the New Testament writers often admonish believers to avoid these sins since such activities are not proper for believers (5:3).

The reason we must avoid these vices is because we have been given a new nature and new identity in Christ. This new identity provides the reason we *must* reject sin and the ability and strength so that we *can* reject sin. Jesus says, "Apart from me you can do nothing" (John 15:5). On our own strength we will fall and we will fail. God calls us to do what we cannot do, but he provides the ability to do what he calls. Apart from the life-giving power of the Spirit, we have no desire, motivation, or power to overcome sin. Before we were "darkness," and now we are "light" (5:8). We have been given a new nature that includes new desires, motivations, and power. Brothers and sisters, before a change in behavior is possible, a change in identity is needed. And once a change in identity is given, a change in behavior is expected.

PRAY

O God, I rejoice that in Christ I am a new creature—
old things have passed and the new has come.
In light of this truth, help me to avoid sins that defame
Christ and that are not fitting for a follower of Christ.
Instead, fill my heart with thanksgiving and joy. Amen.

STUDY IT FURTHER

1. In this passage, Paul mentions that those who are sexually immoral, impure, or covetous will not enter God's kingdom (5:5). Study 1 Corinthians 6:9–10 and Galatians 5:19–21 for other categories of individuals who will be excluded.

2. Throughout the New Testament, God's people are exhorted to flee from sin. Study the following passages to see where we are commanded to flee sexual immorality (Acts 15:20; 1 Cor 6:18; Col 3:5; 1 Thess 4:3; Heb 12:16; 13:4), greed or the love of money (Col 3:5; 1 Tim 6:9–11; Heb 13:5), and unwholesome speech (Col 4:6; 1 Tim 4:12; Titus 2:8; see also Prov 4:24). How has the Spirit strengthened you in times of temptation?

3. Although the phrase "the kingdom of Christ and God" (5:5) is unique to the New Testament, see 2 Timothy 4:1, 18 and 2 Peter 1:11, where reference is made to Christ's kingdom. What do these references regarding Christ's kingdom reveal to us about the Trinity?

Day 29

Ephesians 5:7–14

READ

Therefore do not become partners with them;
for at one time you were darkness, but now you are light in the Lord. Walk as children of light (for the fruit of light is found in all that is good and right and true), and try to discern what is pleasing to the Lord. Take no part in the unfruitful works of darkness, but instead expose them. For it is shameful even to speak of the things that they do in secret. But when anything is exposed by the light, it becomes visible, for anything that becomes visible is light. Therefore it says,
"Awake, O sleeper, and arise
from the dead, and Christ will shine on you."

MEDITATE

The Bible often offers contrasts. Jesus is the true Christ (Messiah), but we are told to beware of false christs (Matt 24:24). Jesus is the good shepherd, but there are thieves and hired hands who don't care for the sheep (John 10:10–14). God is light, and darkness is not found in him (1 John 1:5). In this passage, Paul also uses the imagery of light and darkness, not in relation to God, but in relation to believers. Indeed, as children of God, we are exhorted to "walk as children of light" (5:8). But what does this mean?

Walking in the light means avoiding the darkness: The first step of walking in the light is to avoid the darkness by not "becoming partners" (5:7) with those who might try to deceive us with empty words (5:6). As believers, we should not associate or embrace the ungodly lifestyle of non-Christians. Paul is not referring to some form of radical separation from the world (see 1 Cor 5:9–10). Rather, believers cannot embrace the immoral lifestyle associated with such false teaching. This worldview and conduct must be avoided. Paul also states that we should "take no part in the unfruitful works of darkness" (5:11; see also Rom 13:12). We cannot be partners with those who walk in darkness if we are to imitate God who is light. Indeed, we ourselves "were darkness," but now we are "light in the Lord" (5:8). Thus, participation with false teachers and their lifestyle is inconsistent with our new identity in Christ.

Walking in the light means embracing what is right: Paul goes beyond telling us to avoid sin by telling us to actively embrace that which is "good and right and true" (5:9). Our rejection of the darkness means we choose instead the "fruit of light" (5:8). When we receive new life in Christ, God empowers us to produce characteristics that are found in himself. This fruit is not the means by which God accepts us but the by-product of being united to Christ by faith. Walking in the light also means seeking to do "what is pleasing to the Lord" (5:10). It should be our goal to please our Lord in all circumstances.

Walking in the light means exposing the darkness: Sin should not only be avoided and rejected; it should be exposed (5:11, 13). Paul is not referring to exposing sins of non-Christians but sins committed by those in the church. It is assumed and expected that unbelievers will sin and walk in darkness. But Paul is writing to believers who are called to walk in the light. Furthermore, we have an obligation to expose deeds of darkness with the hope that those who have gone astray will, like the prodigal son, come to their senses and repent. The reason that such exposure needs to take place is because it is shameful even to speak of such deeds that are committed in secret (5:11). But when these deeds are brought into the light, they become visible. The light of the gospel has the power to transform sinners caught in the darkness. Some will accept the reproof and exposure brought about by the gospel and become light in the Lord.

REFLECT ON CHRIST

Twice Paul references the Lord in this passage: "you are light in the Lord" (5:8) and "discern what is pleasing to the Lord" (5:10). As is true with nearly all the references to the Lord in Ephesians, these refer to the Lord Jesus. Notice that Paul does not state that we were once *in* darkness but are now *in* the light. Rather, he writes that we *were* darkness and now *are* light. We have been given a new status, and this status is possible because we are "light *in the Lord*" (5:8, emphasis added). Our union with Christ makes the decisive difference regarding our new state. Now, we consciously desire to make decisions that are "pleasing to the Lord" (5:10). Because our allegiance has changed, our actions change as well.

The final verse of this passage says, "Awake, O sleeper, and arise from the dead, and Christ will shine on you" (5:14). This is a call for those in the church who are slumbering in moral indolence to wake up and flee from sin and to pursue righteousness. It is a call for disobedient and wayward believers to turn to Christ. The promise is that "Christ will shine on you" (5:14).

He will encourage, lead, support, and sustain those who look to him for strength.

APPLY GOD'S WORD

Paul makes the claim that we *are* light, and he commands us to "walk as children of light" (5:8). The order here is intentional: because of who we are in Christ, we can (and must) strive to become what we already are in him. Our lifestyle should conform to the reality of being a new person in Christ. But the power needed to live a transformed life can only come through a relationship with the risen Lord.

What should be done when we don't display the fruit of life but instead produce the fruit of darkness? Paul calls us to bring what is shameful into the light (5:13). Only then is it visible and able to be transformed by the light of Christ. We have an obligation to expose blatant and disgraceful sins that are shameful even to mention in order to awaken those who are slumbering to Christ's light shining on them (5:14). The light of God's word illuminates the darkness and exposes it. We must do this with wisdom and grace as Paul writes, "Brothers, if anyone is caught in any transgression, you who are spiritual should restore him in a spirit of gentleness. Keep watch on yourself, lest you too be tempted" (Gal 6:1).

PRAY

Lord, at one time I was darkness, but you have made me
light. Because of who I now am, help me
to avoid partnering with those who have turned
from your ways and help me to walk as your child,
embracing all that is good and right
and true. For the sake of your name. Amen.

STUDY IT FURTHER

1. The terms "darkness" and "light" are used metaphorically to communicate a moral state of sin or evil versus one of goodness and righteousness. Study the passages where this imagery is used by Paul (Rom 13:12–13; 2 Cor 4:4–6; 6:14; Col 1:12–13; 1 Thess 5:5; and 1 Tim 6:16).

2. The verb translated "discern" means "put to the test," "examine," or "approve." See Romans 2:18; 12:2; Galatians 6:4; Philippians 1:10; and 1 Thessalonians 5:21, where this term is also used, noting specifically what believers are to discern.

3. See the following verses where the verb "expose" (5:11) is used by Paul to rebuke errant members of the community (1 Tim 5:20; 2 Tim 4:2; and Titus 1:9, 13; see also Matt 18:15; Gal 6:1; Rev 3:19). When have you needed a word of rebuke yourself or called out the sin in someone else's life? How did God work through this scenario?

Day 30

Ephesians 5:15–17

READ

Look carefully then how you walk, not as unwise but as wise,
making the best use of the time,
because the days are evil. Therefore do not be foolish,
but understand what the will of the Lord is.

MEDITATE

Often a parent calls out to a child as they head out the door, "Be careful!" Why? Because fathers and mothers love their children and want what is best for them, not for them to make foolish decisions. In the same way, Paul, under the inspiration of the Holy Spirit, speaks God's word of concern to us when he says, "Be very careful, then, how you live" (NIV). This word of caution is not to stifle us but to help us flourish. So how are we to live or walk in this world?

Walk carefully with wisdom: The first directive is that we should live "not as unwise but as wise" (5:15). Our behavior as believers should be characterized by wisdom. Earlier, Paul prayed that God would give us "the Spirit of wisdom and of revelation in the knowledge of him" (1:17). But what is wisdom?

It is "the quality of discerning what is true, what is ethically right, and what should be done in different situations."[5] More than knowledge, it is acquiring situational discretion in life. It is knowing to do the right thing, and then having the skill and desire to live according to that knowledge.

One of the ways we walk wisely is by "making the best use of the time" (5:16). That is, walking with wisdom means that we take full advantage of every opportunity to do the right thing that comes our way. Sitting back and trying to avoid sin and evil is not enough. We should proactively seek to use our gifts in a way that helps further God's kingdom. Why? Paul tells us that it is "because the days are evil" (5:16). Paul believed that we are living in the last days. This age (the present evil age) will someday give way to the coming age (when the kingdom of God comes in its fullness in the new heavens and the new earth). One day, Jesus the Messiah will return and subdue all his enemies under his feet, defeat death, and make all things new. But until then, Paul exhorts us to carefully walk with wisdom, taking every opportunity to do the right thing.

Walk carefully with understanding: The second way that we are to walk carefully is "not to be foolish, but understand what the will of the Lord is" (5:17). Negatively, we are *not* to be foolish. Positively, we are to understand (and do!) the Lord's will. As God's people, we are expected to diligently discover God's moral purpose, which he has already revealed in his word, and apply that knowledge to our lives. This type of understanding is cognitive knowledge combined with applied knowledge.

---

5. R. P. Nettelhorst, "Wisdom," in *Lexham Theological Wordbook*, ed. D. Mangum, D. R. Brown, R. Klippenstein, and R. Hurst (Lexham, 2014).

REFLECT ON CHRIST

Walking with wisdom and understanding is to walk as Christ walked. He taught with the wisdom of God. He had a message greater than Jonah's and a wisdom greater than King Solomon's (Matt 12:41–42). He was the embodiment of wisdom, since he had a unique relationship with the Father (Matt 11:27). Paul explicitly calls Jesus the "wisdom of God" (1 Cor 1:24; see also 1:30). Indeed, the wisdom of God was personified by Jesus and his death on the cross—an act that seems foolish to the world (1 Cor 2:7–8).

Paul notes that believers should understand "the will of the Lord" (Eph 5:17). Interestingly, Paul normally speaks of God's will, but here he refers to the Lord's will. For example, Romans 12:2 states, "Be transformed by the renewal of your mind, that by testing you may discern what is the will of God." In Ephesians, "Lord" is almost always a reference to Christ, as it is here. Thus, Paul gives this appeal a Christ-centered focus. Because we have "learned Christ" (4:20) and now are "light in the Lord" (5:8), we can pursue that which is "pleasing to the Lord" (5:10) by doing "the will of the Lord" (5:17). To walk wisely means to walk as Jesus walked according to his word.

APPLY GOD'S WORD

As believers, we are called to live differently than the world. The world is under the sway of the evil one and does his will. We are to walk with wisdom and understanding and follow God's will. We have a different master and therefore a different set of directives. But this is not always easy for us. Consequently, this passage reminds us to pay careful attention to how we live. The siren call of the world can easily draw us from our devotion to Christ and the way of wisdom. We need constant reminders and encouragement to walk on the straight and narrow path that leads to life. Because Jesus is the wisdom of God personified, the wise person will heed his words (Matt 7:24). We need to make "the best use of the time because the days are evil" (Eph 5:16). Too often we waste our time, being allured by the trappings of this world. What do you fill your time with? Are these things consistent with the Lord's will? Some things may not be sinful, but they may not be a wise use of the precious time and resources God has given us. What is one decision you can make today that would be considered a *wise* decision?

PRAY

O Lord, I sometimes make unwise and foolish decisions.
I am thankful for the forgiveness I have in Christ.
By your Spirit, enable me to walk with wisdom
and understanding. Keep me from evil and help me
to use my time wisely as I seek to do your will. Amen.

STUDY IT FURTHER

1. Paul instructs us to walk with wisdom. See Ephesians 1:8, 17; and 3:10, and note how wisdom is referenced in those verses. Why is wisdom a critical thing to have as children of God?

2. Old Testament wisdom literature contains many admonitions to live not as fools but to seek God's wisdom. For example, the Bible declares, "The fear of the Lord is the beginning of wisdom" (Prov 9:10; see also Ps 111:10; Prov 1:7; 15:33). Read Proverbs 10:23; 23:9; and 24:7, and note what it means to walk with wisdom and not as a fool.

3. Paul often contrasts the present evil age with the age to come. Study Romans 8:18; Galatians 1:4; Ephesians 2:2; and 6:13 to see the contrast between these two ages. How does the future age inform the way we live in the present age?

Day 31

Ephesians 5:18–21

READ

And do not get drunk with wine, for that is debauchery,
but be filled with the Spirit, addressing one another
in psalms and hymns and spiritual songs, singing
and making melody to the Lord with your heart,
giving thanks always and for everything
to God the Father in the name of our Lord Jesus Christ,
submitting to one another out of reverence for Christ.

MEDITATE

When someone drinks too much wine, it causes them to get drunk (and in the ancient world—as in the modern world—drunkenness was often associated with wild and immoral living). Being "filled" with wine influences one's behavior. It causes a person to talk differently, respond differently, and act differently. Similarly, when someone is filled with the Spirit (or filled *by* the Spirit), it affects the way a person talks, responds, and acts. Thus, we are commanded to avoid being under the influence of "spirits" and instead be under the influence of *the*

Spirit. How can we tell if a person is filled with the Spirit? Paul lists three characteristics of such a person.

A Spirit-filled person sings praises to God: First, Paul mentions that those under the Spirit's influence are engaged in singing "psalms and hymns and spiritual songs, singing and making melody" in their hearts (5:19). It is good and right that Christians sing in worship services. This is not just a time-filler or preparation to hear the sermon. It is an act of worship and a natural response to the supernatural filling of God's Spirit. Of course, such singing will not be limited to corporate worship—but it certainly is not less than that. Paul also indicates that two dimensions are involved in our singing: a vertical and a horizontal. The vertical dimension relates to God. We sing "to the Lord" (5:19), who is worthy of our praise. He is the almighty creator and redeemer. He chooses us, redeems us, adopts us, and seals us with his Spirit. But also note the horizontal dimension that Paul emphasizes. In our singing, we also address "one another" (5:19; see also Col 3:16). When we sing to God, we encourage and strengthen the faith of one another.

A Spirit-filled person gives thanks to God for all things: Second, a Spirit-filled person's life is characterized by "giving thanks always and for everything to God the Father in the name of our Lord Jesus Christ" (5:20). When should we give thanks? We should give thanks always, which means that it should be done on a regular basis (not necessarily continually). For what should we give thanks? We should give thanks for everything, which means for all things or in all circumstances, including in our trials and suffering. To whom should we give thanks? We should give thanks to God the Father because he is the creator, sustainer, and redeemer. And how should we give thanks? We should give thanks in the name of our Lord Jesus Christ because Jesus's name (and thus his person and work) is the basis by which we offer thanks and prayers to God.

A Spirit-filled person submits to others: Finally, a Spirit-filled person is someone who submits to others "out of reverence for Christ" (5:21). When we are filled with the Spirit, we are humble and understand that we can learn from others and don't have all the answers. We recognize God's created order in the church and in the family. The motivation for our submission is reverence or holy fear of Christ.

REFLECT ON CHRIST

This passage references "the Lord" (5:19), "the name of our Lord Jesus Christ" (5:20), and "Christ" (5:21), once again emphasizing the centrality of Jesus in Paul's theology. He first notes that our heartfelt singing should be directed to "the Lord" (5:19) since he is our Savior and our redeemer. Pliny, a first-century governor of Bithynia in Asia Minor, described Christians as worshiping and singing to Jesus. He stated that they "regularly assembled on a certain day before daybreak. They recited a hymn antiphonally to Christ as (their) God."[6] Pliny, though he was not a Christian, portrayed the early church as singing hymns to Christ the Lord.

Second, not only is our singing directed to Christ, but our thanksgiving to the Father is "in the name of our Lord Jesus Christ" (5:20). It is only through Christ that we have access to the Father through the power of the Spirit. Finally, we submit to one another "out of reverence for Christ" (5:20). Because Christ is the Lord of the church, Lord of the family, and Lord of society, we should not only humbly submit to those he has placed

---

6. *The Letters of the Younger Pliny* 10.96, cited from Craig Evans, *Ancient Texts for New Testament Studies: A Guide to Background Literature* (Hendrickson, 2005), 299.

in authority over us, but we should freely submit to others in the body of Christ, allowing them to speak into our lives.

APPLY GOD'S WORD

The Spirit of God empowers us to obey the ethical injunctions that Paul provides in this passage. Just as being under the influence of wine leads to a certain type of behavior, being under the influence of the Spirit leads to God-ordained behavior. The Spirit enables us to "put to death the deeds of the body" (Rom 8:13). When we walk by the Spirit, we are able to avoid gratifying "the desires of the flesh" (Gal 5:16). Similar to God's Spirit filling the tabernacle and temple in the Old Testament, the Spirit of God fills and indwells us, permitting us to walk in holiness. Indeed, we are called to be holy just as God is holy (1 Pet 1:16). The evidence of walking a Spirit-filled life is singing heartfelt praise to the Lord, giving thanks in all circumstances, and willingly and humbly submitting to others. Pray about which of these three areas in your life you need to focus on so that you can work to bring it more in line with a Spirit-filled life.

PRAY

O God, fill me with the Spirit of Christ so that I sing to you freely, give thanks to you regularly, and submit to others willingly. Keep me from the allures of this world that lead me away from you. To your name be the glory, and the power, and the praise, both now and forevermore. Amen.

STUDY IT FURTHER

1. Paul indicates that the problem with drunkenness is that it leads to debauchery (5:18). The term "debauchery" refers to "behavior which shows lack of concern or thought for the consequences of an action."[7] Also see Titus 1:6 and 1 Peter 4:4, where this term is used. Are there areas in your life that could lead to such behavior if left unchecked?

2. The phrase "be filled with the Spirit" (5:18) could also be translated "be filled by the Spirit." The first translation relates to the content of that with which believers are filled, whereas the second refers to the agent who fills believers. If the latter option is preferred, then what is the content of that with which believers are filled? See Ephesians 4:13 for a possible option.

3. Read Colossians 3:16, noting how that verse is similar to Ephesians 5:19 and how it is different. What do you think it means to "let the word of Christ dwell in you richly"?

---

7. Johannes P. Louw, and Eugene A. Nida, *Greek-English Lexicon of the New Testament Based on Semantic Domains*, 2 vols. (United Bible Societies, 1988), §88.96.

Day 32

Ephesians 5:22–24

READ

Wives, submit to your own husbands, as to the Lord.
For the husband is the head of the wife even as Christ
is the head of the church, his body,
and is himself its Savior. Now as the church
submits to Christ, so also wives should submit
in everything to their husbands.

MEDITATE

Beginning in this passage, Paul addresses various groups in the church: wives and husbands (5:22–33), children and parents (6:1–4), and slaves and masters (6:5–9). The gospel affects the way we relate to others, including how spouses relate to one another. In these verses (5:22–24), we will highlight the role of the wife. The primary directive that Paul offers to wives is that they should submit to their husbands (see 5:22, 24, 33). Although often misunderstood and abused, submission is the voluntary act of yielding to the leadership of another. In the context of marriage, it is something that is willingly offered, not something that is demanded. It also does not reflect the worth or value of someone. Christ willingly submits to the Father and yet is equal to the Father as the Second Person of the Trinity (1 Cor 15:28). Submission does not denote inferiority but relates to God's design in marriage. Women and men are equal in value and worth since both are created in God's image. Based on God's creational design, however, men and women have different roles in the marriage relationship. Paul clarifies what this submission entails.

Wives should submit to their own husbands: Because the terms for "wife" and "husband" in the Greek language could be rendered "woman" and "man," it is possible that Paul is speaking broadly of society and is not limiting his statements to marriage. However, because he states that women/wives must submit to their "own" men/husbands, we know he is referring to wives and husbands (5:22). Thus, a wife is not expected to submit to men in general or to someone else's husband but specifically to her own husband.

Wives should submit as to the Lord: Paul uses a comparison in order to show the significance of his command and to provide motivation for submission. A wife should submit to her husband "as to the Lord" (5:22). In submitting to her husband, a wife is simultaneously submitting to Christ the Lord. When we love others, we are displaying love to God. Similarly, submitting to others signifies our willingness to submit to the Lord.

Wives should submit to their husbands because they are the heads: Paul offers a reason as to why wives should submit: "For the husband is the head of the wife" (5:23). Because God has given headship and leadership to the husband in the marriage relationship, a wife should submit to him.

Wives should submit as the church submits to Christ: Just as the church (God's people) should voluntarily submit to Christ and his word, so wives should freely submit to their husbands.

Wives should submit in everything: This statement should not be taken absolutely. The Bible often gives commands or makes statements without providing exceptions. Jesus says, "Ask, and it will be given to you" (Matt 7:7), but we don't always get what we ask for because there are obvious exceptions, some even stated elsewhere in Scripture. A wife should not submit to her husband in matters that are sinful, harmful, or contrary to God's commands (see Acts 5:29). But in general, a wife should look for ways to affirm and support her husband.

Wives should submit respectfully: In 5:33, after a lengthy section on the role of the husband in marriage, Paul returns to the role of wives. This time, he notes that wives should respect their husbands. The verb translated "respect" is often rendered "fear" in the New Testament, but the meaning is not that a wife should live in fear of her husband. Rather, a wife should have reverential respect for him.

REFLECT ON CHRIST

Christ is lord over individuals, over families, and over the church. When Paul informs wives to submit to their husbands "as to the Lord" (5:22), he brings a gospel-focused and Christ-centered approach to marriage. Ultimately, we can't comply with the commands of Scripture out of sheer willpower. Such an approach will not get us far. Instead, we strive to honor others because we hear Jesus say, "As you did it to one of the least of these my brothers, you did it to me" (Matt 25:40). As we have freely received, we freely give.

The marriage relationship is patterned after Christ and the church. Christ is described as the head and Savior of the church (5:23). As head, he possesses authority over the church, which is also described as his body. And he is the Savior of the church, because he redeemed the church by his sacrifice. Because of this relationship, the church is to submit to Christ. Similarly, because the husband is head of the wife (notice that he is never said to be the savior of the wife), the wife is to submit to him.

APPLY GOD'S WORD

Submission is not easy. From the curse of Genesis 3, it appears willing submission is made difficult after the fall. God says to Eve: "Your desire shall be contrary to your husband, but he shall rule over you" (Gen 3:16). Perhaps this is why Paul provides us the proper motivation for submission: "as to the Lord" (5:22) and "as the church submits to Christ" (5:24). Wives, do you seek to serve your husband with a Christ-centered motivation? Do you look for ways to show respect and honor to him? Husbands, are you tempted to demand that your wife submits? Is that consistent with this passage or with how Christ relates to the church?

PRAY

O Jesus, I praise you because you are the head and Savior of the church. As such, help me to submit to you willingly and gladly. You are without fault and perfect in all your ways. But Lord, also help me to submit to those in authority over me—those who are not without fault or perfect. May I serve others with the mindset that I am serving you. Amen.

STUDY IT FURTHER

1. For other exhortations to wives, see Colossians 3:18; Titus 2:5; and 1 Peter 3:1–5. What do these passages include that are not found in Ephesians 5:22–24?

2. There is debate as to whether the term "head" (*kephalē*) refers to "authority over" or "source." Read Ephesians 1:22, and 4:15 where the term is used in reference to Christ. What meaning fits best in these passages?

3. Read 1 Corinthians 11:3–12 and 1 Timothy 2:11–14. What is the basis on which the leadership role is given to husbands?

Day 33

Ephesians 5:25–33

READ

Husbands, love your wives, as Christ loved the church and gave himself up for her, that he might sanctify her, having cleansed her by the washing of water with the word, so that he might present the church to himself in splendor, without spot or wrinkle or any such thing, that she might be holy and without blemish. In the same way husbands should love their wives as their own bodies. He who loves his wife loves himself. For no one ever hated his own flesh, but nourishes and cherishes it, just as Christ does the church, because we are members of his body. "Therefore a man shall leave his father and mother and hold fast to his wife, and the two shall become one flesh." This mystery is profound, and I am saying that it refers to Christ and the church. However, let each one of you love his wife as himself, and let the wife see that she respects her husband.

MEDITATE

After instructing the wives to submit to their husbands, Paul turns to the husbands and urges them to love their wives. When compared with first-century Greco-Roman literature, Paul's focus on the need for husbands to love their wives is unexpected. The command to love—which is emphasized, being mentioned three times (5:25, 28, 33)—is a command to follow the way of Christ.

Husbands should love their wives sacrificially: Just as Christ gave himself up for the church (5:25), husbands should be willing to serve their wives, sacrificing their rights and interests. Of course, Christ did not merely give up his rights, he gave up his life. His love was sacrificial in the deepest sense. Husbands are not asked to give up their lives for their wives. But they are asked to take on the mind of Christ and follow in his self-sacrificing love—a love that is willing to sacrifice in order to protect and care for their brides.

Husbands should love their wives unconditionally: Christ loved the church (made up of redeemed sinners) even when she was not worthy. Similarly, a husband should love his wife whether she is deserving of his love or not. Christ loved us while we were his enemies, sinners, and ungodly. His love is not determined by our conduct. Just as Hosea kept loving and pursuing Gomer, even though she was unfaithful, husbands should love and pursue their wives.

Husbands should love their wives purposefully: Just as Jesus sanctifies, cleanses, and presents his bride as pure, so husbands should seek to lead their wives with the purpose of helping them conform to the image of Christ (5:26–27). Jesus sanctifies his bride (the church) "having cleansed her by the washing of water with the word" (5:26)—that is, the church is made holy and purified by the cleansing power of the gospel. The end result of this sanctifying work is "so that he might present the church to himself in splendor" (5:27). Someday, when Christ returns, he will present his bride "without spot or wrinkle or any such thing" (5:27). Similarly, a husband should seek to live with his wife in such a way that she grows more and more into the likeness of Christ.

Husbands should love their wives affectionately: Christ loves the church by nourishing and cherishing her. In the same way, husbands should lavishly provide for their wives (5:28–32). Just as it is natural for a man to nurture and protect himself, a husband is to love his wife. Because the husband and wife become "one flesh" (5:31), when the husband loves his wife, in that sense he is also loving himself. Paul is urging a husband to be attentive to the needs of his wife. A husband should seek to communicate with and understand his wife so that he can adequately know her needs and care for her affectionately.

REFLECT ON CHRIST

The marriage relationship reflects something deeper than simply a man and woman's love for each other. It is patterned after and reflects Christ's love for the church. Both the foundation and the goal of marriage are based on this relationship. Christ loves the church, sacrificed himself for her, sanctifies her, cleanses her, nourishes and cherishes her, and will someday present her blameless. Marriage is not merely an end in itself. It points to a greater relationship, a greater love, a greater future. The apostle John writes, "Blessed are those who are invited to the marriage supper of the Lamb" (Rev 19:9). God's people are blessed because they will fellowship with God for eternity. In 1 Corinthians, Jesus is called both the second Adam and the last Adam (1 Cor 15:45–47). Just as the first Adam was joined to his wife and they became one flesh (Gen 2:24), so the last or second Adam (Christ) is joined to his bride (the church) so that his people are united with him. Therefore, Christ's love for the church is not patterned after the marriage relationship between a man and a wife, but the marriage relationship is patterned after Christ and the church. This is a great mystery indeed.

APPLY GOD'S WORD

Loving someone all day long, every day is not always easy. But we find strength and motivation for loving our spouse in the example of Christ. We love because he first loved us (1 John 4:19). When we reflect on the love, patience, and forgiveness that Christ offers us in the gospel, we should likewise be willing to love, be patient, and forgive others. We have spots and blemishes, and yet we receive complete and unconditional acceptance. Husbands, are you willing to love your wife sacrificially? To lay aside your rights and preferences for her? Are you willing to love her unconditionally? To love her even if she does not deserve to receive your love? Are you willing to love her purposefully? To love her in such a way that she grows in her likeness to Christ? And are you willing to love her affectionately? To love her by nourishing and cherishing her above all others? What can you do today to show her the type of love that you yourself have received from Christ?

PRAY

Dear Lord, because you have loved love me sacrificially,
unconditionally, purposefully, and affectionately,
help me to offer that type of love to people around me.
Jesus, you are the perfect husband, so I will
look to you as a guide to help me love others
as you have loved your church. Amen.

STUDY IT FURTHER

1. In Ephesians 5:26, Paul says that Christ cleanses the church by the "washing of the water with the word." The Greek term for "word" is (*rhēma*) in this passage. Based on the following passages, what does the "word" refer to here (Rom 10:8, 17; Eph 6:17; Heb 6:5; 1 Pet 1:25)?

2. It is likely that Christ's presentation of his glorious bride, the church, will take place at his second coming (5:27). Read 2 Corinthians 4:14 and Colossians 1:22, 28, where the same verb ("present") is used in a similar context.

3. Paul calls the Christ-church relationship a great or profound "mystery" (5:32), meaning that some aspect of God's plan was once hidden but is now revealed in Jesus. For more texts relating to this mystery, see Romans 16:25; Ephesians 1:9; 3:3–4, 9; 6:19. What do you think this "mystery" is?

Day 34

Ephesians 6:1–4

READ

Children, obey your parents in the Lord,
for this is right. "Honor your father and mother"
(this is the first commandment with a promise),
"that it may go well with you
and that you may live long in the land."
Fathers, do not provoke your children to anger, but bring
them up in the discipline and instruction of the Lord.

MEDITATE

After giving instruction to wives and husbands, Paul turns to the relationship of children and their parents.

Children should obey and honor their parents: Noticeably, Paul asks children to submit to their parents and to obey them. The verb "obey" is stronger than the verb "submit." Submission is a voluntary act among equals. Obedience is a mandatory act in respect to a superior. Wives are asked to submit to their husbands, but children are exhorted to obey their parents. The term used for "children" could also apply to adult children. In this context, however, Paul addresses those children who are still in the process of being trained by their parents (6:4). And yet these children also seem old enough to comprehend their relationship with the Lord (6:1), and they are addressed as responsible members of the congregation. The phrase "in the Lord" modifies the verb "obey." In this context, Paul is addressing Christian children (though non-Christian children also need to obey their parents). The implication is that children need to obey their parents whether their parents are Christians or not (of course, there are always exceptions since a child should not obey a parent if the child is asked or expected to sin). The rationale for this command is that it is right (6:1). That is, this command should be obeyed because it is fitting or proper and according to God's creational design.

Paul then cites the fifth commandment to support his injunction for children to obey their parents: "Honor your father and your mother" (6:2). To obey one's parents is a way of honoring them. Paul adds that "this is the first commandment with a promise" (6:2). The promise given includes a twofold blessing: "that it may go well with you and that you may live long in the land" (6:3). The first blessing relates to one's general prosperity. The second, "that you may live long in the land," includes the blessing of life on the earth.

Fathers should not provoke but train their children: Here, Paul directs his focus specifically on fathers since fathers were typically responsible for the education and the discipline of their children. He first provides a prohibition and then a positive command. First, fathers should not provoke their children to anger (6:4). They are not to cause them to become angry by excessive discipline, unreasonable demands, or abusive actions (see Col 3:21). Second, fathers are to "bring [their children] up in the discipline and instruction of the Lord" (6:4). Just as a husband "nourishes" (same word as "bring up") his own body (5:29), so a father should seek to nourish his children, cultivating them to grow and mature in the ways of the Lord. Specifically, fathers are to nourish their children in the discipline and instruction of Christ. In our modern context, these admonishments would apply to both fathers and mothers. They are to educate, train, and verbally instruct and correct their children. Children are a gift from God and have been entrusted to parents. Parents are to raise their children with the wisdom of Christ.

REFLECT ON CHRIST

Although Paul's focus is on giving instructions to children ("obey" and "honor") and to fathers ("do not provoke" and "bring them up"), Christ is still prominent in this passage. Children are to obey their parents "in the Lord" (6:1), which is a reference to Christ. Children are to obey their parents because their parents occupy a place of authority over them and out of love and reverence for Christ. Ultimately, their obedience is an overflow of discipleship. It is done as to the Lord. The promise of the command ("that it may go well with you and that you may live long in the land") also points us to Christ, since all the promises of God are "yes" and "amen" in him. There is no blessing that we receive that was not secured for us by Christ.

Paul notes that fathers are to bring their children up in the training and instruction of the Lord (6:4). The manner and the content of a parent's instruction should be thoroughly Christ-centered. It is easy for parents to revert to their own wisdom or own desires, but Paul makes it clear that parents are to raise their children with instruction that comes from Christ and is prescribed by him.

APPLY GOD'S WORD

What does it mean to walk with wisdom (5:15) and to be filled with the Spirit (5:18) as a follower of Christ? This passage offers practical guidance for what that entails. Our obedience to Christ is often parallel to our obedience to our family members. If we want to obey Christ and walk in wisdom and in the Spirit, then we should obey our parents "in the Lord" (6:1). We obey as part of our commitment to Christ. If we want to obey Christ and walk in wisdom and in the Spirit, then we should raise our children in the ways of Jesus.

Paul offers motivation for our obedience, especially with how children should obey and honor their parents. They should obey because it is right (6:1), because God commanded it (in the fifth commandment), and because there is great reward (6:3).

What is one thing you can do today to obey and honor your parents? Likewise, what is one thing you can do today that signifies that you are seeking to bring up your children in the discipline and instruction of the Lord (if applicable)?

PRAY

Father, your word is true, help me to love it.
Jesus, your ways are right, help me to follow them.
Spirit, your witness is compelling,
help me to surrender to it. Amen.

STUDY IT FURTHER

1. The fifth commandment is cited five other times in the New Testament. Read the following passages, noting the context of the citation (Matt 15:4; 19:19; Mark 7:10; 10:19; and Luke 18:20). Do you think it is significant that Ephesians is the only citation of the fifth commandment that includes the promise? Why or why not?

2. Exodus 20:12 states, "Honor your father and your mother, that your days may be long in the land that the LORD your God is giving you." Why do you think that the final phrase ("that the LORD your God is giving you") is not quoted by Paul in Ephesians 6:3?

3. What would it mean for a parent to "provoke" their children?

Day 35

Ephesians 6:5–9

READ

Bondservants, obey your earthly masters with fear
and trembling, with a sincere heart, as you would Christ,
not by the way of eye-service, as people-pleasers,
but as bondservants of Christ, doing the will of God from
the heart, rendering service with a good will
as to the Lord and not to man, knowing that whatever good
anyone does, this he will receive back from
the Lord, whether he is a bondservant or is free. Masters, do
the same to them, and stop your threatening, knowing
that he who is both their Master and yours
is in heaven, and that there is no partiality with him.

MEDITATE

After addressing wives and husbands and then children and parents, Paul now turns to bondservants (slaves) and masters. Slavery was common in the ancient world and was accepted as a part of culture. In Galatians 3:28, Paul indicates that—when it comes to the promise of the gospel to save those who believe—"there is neither slave nor free." Yet, Paul's words in Galatians don't absolve all cultural and societal norms. Within those systems (some just and some unjust), followers of Christ need to prioritize the gospel and not their own personal rights or preferences.

Slaves should obey their masters: The main command that Paul offers is for slaves to "obey [their] earthly masters" (6:5). Although slaves were not typically addressed in household codes, Paul doesn't skip them. He treats all levels of society as equal members of Christ's church who have an obligation to live out the gospel wherever they are. The phrase "earthly masters" stands in contrast to God, the heavenly Master (6:9).

Paul provides six qualifying phrases that specify the manner in which slaves are to obey their masters. First, they are to obey "with fear and trembling" (6:5), indicating the respect that should be given. Second, they are to obey "with a sincere heart" (6:5), signifying integrity and purity. Third, they are to obey "as [they] would Christ" (6:5), emphasizing that obedience offered to others is ultimately obedience to Christ, our true Master. Fourth, slaves are to obey "not by the way of eye-service, as people-pleasers" (6:6), demonstrating consistent obedience is done to please God. Fifth, they are to obey "as bondservants of Christ, doing the will of God from the heart" (6:6), implying that one's true and ultimate identity is found in Christ who inspires wholehearted obedience. Sixth, they are to obey "rendering service with a good will" (6:7), suggesting that they should serve with a good attitude and serve with eagerness since their service ultimately is "to the Lord and not to man" (6:7).

Verse 8 provides the rationale as to why slaves should obey their masters: "knowing that whatever good anyone does, this he will receive back from the Lord." Obedient, wholehearted service will be rewarded at the last judgment by the heavenly

Master. All (whether bondservant or free) will be judged and rewarded equally because there is no favoritism with God.

Masters should treat their slaves properly: After addressing bondservants, Paul exhorts masters to "do the same" (6:9) to their slaves. This parity of commands between slaves and masters would have been viewed as shocking to many of this time period. This command includes the attitudes of masters and their actions since they are to *do* the same. Even if there is not a symmetrical relationship (different social statuses), there is a reciprocal relationship; slaves and masters are to treat each other appropriately, rendering such obedience to the Lord.

Proper treatment means that masters should not threaten their slaves. All forms of verbal (and physical) abuse must be rejected by Christ-followers. Why? First, they will be held accountable for their actions ("he who is both their Master and yours is in heaven"). Second, the Lord does not judge with partiality ("there is no partiality with him"). Social status does not give someone an advantage before the judgment of God. This reality should influence how we treat others.

REFLECT ON CHRIST

For a passage dealing with slaves and masters, this text is replete with references to Christ. Specifically, "Christ" is referenced twice (6:5, 6) and "Lord/Master" (same word in Greek) is referenced three times (6:7, 8, 9). Every verse in this passage has a reference to Jesus. First, Christ is the focus of our obedience (6:5). We obey others as we are obeying Christ himself. Second, we obey because we are servants of Christ (6:6). Our obedience flows from the fact that Christ has purchased our freedom and we belong to him. Third, we obey with the right attitude ("with a good will") since our service is ultimately to Christ and not to man. Fourth, regardless of our standing in society, Christ will judge our deeds. And finally, we obey and treat others fairly, because even those who are "lords/masters" have a "Lord/Master" who reigns from heaven and who judges without partiality. Our lives, wherever we are and whoever we are, always stand in relation to Christ. Our attitudes and our actions should be filtered through our relationship with him.

APPLY GOD'S WORD

This passage, although specifically about slaves and masters, has broader implications for all believers. First, it reminds us that we live in a fallen world. Injustice and inequity confront us every day. Christ has come to set us free from the dominion of this world, and he has provided new life and a hope of an everlasting kingdom where righteousness and peace will prevail. Second, this passage reminds us that God is concerned with our actions and our attitudes. In our actions with others, are we serving them "with a sincere heart" (6:5)? In our work for others, could we be described as "people-pleasers" (6:6)? Or do we serve "from the heart" (6:6)? God is concerned with *what* we do and *how* we do it. Third, this passage reminds us that Jesus is our Master and we are his bondservants. No matter the context, our response to the situation is a reflection of our relationship with Christ. All obedience is ultimately obedience to him.

PRAY

O Lord, I approach you with fear and trembling
because you are worthy of all respect and admiration.
Protect me from half-hearted obedience
and from being a people-pleaser.
May I delight in serving you
with a sincere heart, and may I treat those
around me with kindness. Amen.

STUDY IT FURTHER

1. Read 1 Corinthians 2:3; 2 Corinthians 7:15; and Philippians 2:12, noting how the phrase "with fear and trembling" is used. Do these passages help us understand the meaning of this phrase in Ephesians 6:5?

2. If salvation is by grace alone, through faith alone, based on the work of Christ alone (and it is!), then why will believers be judged? (See Rom 2:6; 2 Cor 5:10; Col 3:25; and 1 Pet 5:4.)

3. In this passage, Paul neither explicitly condones nor condemns slavery. And unlike the institution of marriage (5:22–33), he doesn't provide a theological foundation for slavery. How do 1 Corinthians 7:21 and Philemon 15–16 provide further insight into Paul's view of slavery?

Day 36

Ephesians 6:10

READ

Finally, be strong in the Lord and in the strength of his might.

MEDITATE

When my Muslim neighbor came to my house, I knew something must be wrong. At the time, I lived in Southeast Asia and, although this particular neighbor was friendly, he rarely entered our property. In somewhat of a panic, he explained to me that he and his family had been harassed by spirits: the sound of someone knocking on doors or ringing loud bells, an imprint of a body on a bed, and sickness caused by curses. Although his interpretation of these events was that his family was being visited by jinn (good and evil creatures who are invisible to humans), I suggested that such phenomena could be caused by evil spirits or demons. On the outside of the wall around his property was a small Buddhist altar that some neighbors had built and behind his house was a nightclub. He was surrounded by the worship of idols and the indulgence of drugs and immorality. Is it surprising that his family was being tormented by evil spirits?

Be strong in the Lord: As Paul transitions to the conclusion of his letter (signaled by "finally"), he also comes to the climax of the letter. He begins this section (6:10–20) by issuing a general command to "be strong in the Lord." Because this verb is in the passive voice, it could be translated "be strengthened" or "be made strong." The command tells us that this is something that we should do, and the passive voice reminds us that the power to be strong comes from a source outside of ourselves—we must be strong *in the Lord.* Paul earlier prayed that the Ephesian believers might "*be strengthened* with power through his Spirit in [their] inner being" (3:16, emphasis added). He later instructs Timothy, "You then, my child, *be strengthened* by the grace that is in Christ Jesus" (2 Tim 2:1, emphasis added). In the midst of spiritual warfare, the source of our power to fight and stand firm comes through our union with the Lord Jesus Christ.

Be strong by the strength of his might: Although many of us in the West are hesitant to acknowledge the existence of spiritual powers, it is something the biblical authors assumed and something most non-Western cultures accept. How should we respond to this largely unseen reality? We must be prepared. Paul reminds us that our battle is "against the rulers, against the authorities, against the cosmic powers over this present darkness, against the spiritual forces of evil" (6:12). The devil and his minions are well armed and can easily discourage or defeat weary soldiers of the cross. The strength to fight and overcome the enemy is supplied by God. Paul emphatically adds that it is only by "the strength of his might" that we can be in a position to take a stand against the devil. Elsewhere Paul reminds us, "If God is for us, who can be against us?" (Rom 8:31). On our own we are easy prey for the enemy. But when we rely on the strength that God provides, we are more than conquerors.

REFLECT ON CHRIST

Strength or might is something most people desire. Millions of people spend countless hours exercising in an effort to increase their bodily strength. As Christians, we are called to be strong—but our strength does not originate from within. Paul exhorts his readers to find their strength in the Lord, which in this context refers specifically to Christ. God the Son, who is now the exalted Lord seated at the Father's right hand, is the one who strengthens believers.

In several places, Paul reveals that the source of his strength comes from Jesus Christ. In Philippians 4:13, he declares, "I can do all things through Christ who strengthens me" (NKJV). Elsewhere he offers a thanksgiving to Christ: "I thank him who has given me strength, Christ Jesus our Lord, because he judged me faithful, appointing me to his service" (1 Tim 1:12). When Paul was on trial in prison in Rome and all abandoned him, he confidently acknowledged, "But the Lord stood by me and strengthened me, so that through me the message might be fully proclaimed and all the Gentiles might hear it" (2 Tim 4:17). As with Paul, we must realize that our relationship with Christ is the source of our strength.

APPLY GOD'S WORD

What does it mean to be strong with someone else's strength? First, notice that we are given a command. We are exhorted to "be strong." Therefore, this is something we should actively be engaged in doing. This takes intentionality and initiative. We need to wake up each morning and engage our hearts and minds to heed this directive.

Second, we are to look outside of ourselves. Normally when someone tells us to do something, it is because they think we have the ability to do it. But here Paul commands us to be strong with the strength or might of someone else. We must look to Christ to be our strength.

Third, according to the context, the way we seek to be strong in the Lord is by equipping ourselves with the spiritual armor and weaponry that God has provided us. By neglecting the whole armor of God, we are neglecting the strength and power that God has afforded us in Christ. We need God's provision so we can stand against the spiritual onslaught of the devil and his demons. Do truth, righteousness, peace, faith, and salvation characterize your life? Is it evident that God's word, the sword of the Spirit, is a weapon that you know how to appropriately wield?

PRAY

O God, too often I attempt to battle against the enemy in my own strength. Help me to rely on you and your strength. You created the world and all that is in it (Ps 89:11). You sustain the universe by your powerful word (Heb 1:3). You defeated death and the devil by the resurrection of your Son. Help me today to rely on you to become who I am in Christ—more than a conqueror. Amen.

STUDY IT FURTHER

1. In this passage, we are exhorted to find our strength "in the Lord" (6:10). See Ephesians 2:21; 4:1, 17; 5:8; 6:1, 21, where that phrase also refers specifically to Christ. How does Christ strengthen us?

2. How does Jesus's ministry of miracles and healing reveal that our battle is not against flesh and blood?

3. Read Joshua 1:6–9, noting the places where Joshua is exhorted to "be strong." Where was Joshua to find his strength? (See also 1 Sam 30:6 and Zech 10:12.)

Day 37

Ephesians 6:11–13

READ

Put on the whole armor of God, that you may be able to stand against the schemes of the devil. For we do not wrestle against flesh and blood, but against the rulers, against the authorities, against the cosmic powers over this present darkness, against the spiritual forces of evil in the heavenly places. Therefore take up the whole armor of God, that you may be able to withstand in the evil day, and having done all, to stand firm.

MEDITATE

In the previous verse, Paul exhorted us to "be strong in the Lord" (6:10). But what precisely does that look like? How do I know if I am finding strength in the Lord and in his mighty power? Here, Paul gives us practical instructions on how we are to be spiritually equipped to withstand the assault of the enemy.

We need to put on the whole armor of God: The way that we find our strength in the Lord is to "put on the whole armor of God" (6:11). This is not physical armor since our enemy does not have flesh and blood. Rather, Paul is speaking metaphorically of how we need to appropriate our new identity in Christ and the resources that God has made available to each one of us. This armor is described as the "whole" or "full" armor since Paul lists the essential components that a Roman foot soldier would wear into battle and the full protections that such armor supplies. It is the armor "of God" because it is the armor that God provides for us.

We need to stand firm: How does this armor help us? It is given so "that you may be able to stand against the schemes of the devil" (6:11). The devil is waging war against us, and our commander has called us to stand firm against his onslaught. Although this imagery could convey a purely defensive stance (don't retreat or give up ground), more likely it signifies a forceful offensive stance. The threefold repetition of the verb "to stand" (6:11, 13 x2) conveys that this is Paul's main directive. Specifically, this stand is against "the schemes of the devil" (6:11). The implication here is that the devil is actively strategizing as to how to get us to retreat or fall—through desire, difficulties, division, or distractions.

We need to know our enemy: The reason we need to employ divine armor is because of the spiritual nature of the enemy. Paul explains that "we do not wrestle against flesh and blood" (6:12). The imagery of wrestling suggests a close, intense battle. But this is no ordinary battle because it is not against human beings but "against the rulers, against the authorities, against the cosmic powers over this present darkness, against the spiritual forces of evil in the heavenly places" (6:12). Our enemy includes personal, demonic beings that are opposed to God and the expansion of his kingdom.

With a supernatural enemy, it is crucial that we take up the God-given armor. Paul urgently repeats his appeal that we "take up the whole armor of God" (6:13). This time, the reason

Paul provides is "that you may be able to withstand in the evil day" (6:13). Paul was fully aware that there are times in our lives when demonic attacks are at their worst (see 5:16). The importance of being outfitted with God's armor is once again highlighted as Paul states, "and having done all, to stand firm" (6:13). The way we are strong in the Lord and in his mighty power is to put on the armor that he supplies and stand firm, knowing the nature of the enemy.

REFLECT ON CHRIST

This passage does not have any explicit references to Christ. The focus is on the armor of God, which is needed because of the spiritual nature of our enemy. And yet, Christ is at the very heart of this passage. Notice that Paul does not state that the purpose of the armor is so that we might win the victory against the devil. Indeed, the victory has already been secured by Jesus himself. Jesus has already wrestled "against the rulers, against the authorities, against the cosmic powers over this present darkness, against the spiritual forces of evil in the heavenly places" (6:12). According to Paul, Jesus "disarmed the rulers and authorities" by his death and resurrection (Col 2:15). According to the author of Hebrews, it was "through death [that Jesus] might destroy the one who has the power of death, that is, the devil" (Heb 2:14). According to John, "The reason the Son of God appeared was to destroy the works of the devil" (1 John 3:8). The death and resurrection of Jesus secured the victory. We are called to stand firm in the victory that is already guaranteed.

APPLY GOD'S WORD

This passage (6:11–20) is the most sustained treatment of the spiritual battle that wages against us. Paul speaks of the devil

(6:11) and the evil one (6:16) to describe Satan, who is earlier described as "the prince of the power of the air" (2:2). Apparently, Satan is the leader over lesser evil spirits called "rulers," authorities," "cosmic powers," and "spiritual forces" (6:12), all of which are determined to cause harm to God's people. Our response to this reality is to be prepared. Because Satan and his minions are well armed with clever tactics, we must "be strong in the Lord" (6:10). Only by his strength can we fight and overcome the enemy. More specifically, we must stand firm (6:11, 13, 14) with the full armor of God.

Do you acknowledge the spiritual battle that wages around us? Do you look to God for strength each morning and throughout the day? Do you employ the spiritual armor that God has provided? Are you able to successfully stand your ground and not succumb to temptations, trials, troubles, and testings? Today, look to God and his resources to stand in the victory already won by Christ.

PRAY

O God, may I look to you to find my strength.
My enemy can easily overwhelm me. So help me each day
to be mindful of my weakness and employ
the armor that you provide. Thank you
that the victory has been secured through your Son,
and in light of that victory, help me to stand firm. Amen.

STUDY IT FURTHER

1. In 6:10, Paul instructs us to "put on" the divinely supplied armor. Read the following passages and note what else Paul exhorts us to put on (Rom 13:12; Gal 3:27; Eph 4:24; Col 3:10, 12).

2. Paul uses fighting imagery in this passage: armor, schemes, stand/withstand. See Romans 13:12; 2 Corinthians 6:7; 10:3–6; 1 Thessalonians 5:8; 1 Timothy 1:18; and 2 Timothy 2:3–4, where Paul also uses war or battle imagery. Are you prepared to stand against the schemes of the devil?

3. In light of Ephesians 5:16 and Galatians 1:4, what do you think Paul means when he speaks of "the evil day" (6:13)?

Day 38

Ephesians 6:14–17

READ

Stand therefore, having fastened on the belt of truth, and having put on the breastplate of righteousness, and, as shoes for your feet, having put on the readiness given by the gospel of peace. In all circumstances take up the shield of faith, with which you can extinguish all the flaming darts of the evil one; and take the helmet of salvation, and the sword of the Spirit, which is the word of God …

MEDITATE

Standing our ground to fight is not easy, especially when the enemy is more powerful than us. Thankfully, we are neither fighting alone nor by our own strength ("be strong in the Lord and in the strength of his might," 6:10). After explaining the necessity of God's armor, Paul details piece by piece what we should put on.

Stand firm with the belt of truth: The first piece of armor is a belt that represents the truth. The imagery of "fastening" or "girding oneself" signifies preparation for activity or, in this case, a readiness to engage in battle. As we comprehend and affirm the truth of the gospel, we will be strengthened to fight the enemy, standing on God's faithful word.

Stand firm with the breastplate of righteousness: The breastplate covered the chest, protecting it from damaging blows from the enemy. Isaiah 59:17 states that God "put on righteousness as a breastplate." When we imitate the righteous character of God, we are protected from the assault of the enemy.

Stand firm with gospel shoes: The shoes represent "the readiness given by the gospel of peace" (6:15). Paul again alludes to Isaiah, "How beautiful upon the mountains are the feet of him who brings good news, who publishes peace" (52:7). Those who have their feet properly fitted will be equipped and prepared for spiritual warfare and will be able to stand firm through the powerful, peace-giving message of the gospel. But this imagery also suggests a willingness to announce the good news of Jesus and the peace he brings through his work of reconciliation.

Stand firm with the shield of faith: The shield referenced here is not a small, round shield but the large shield carried by Roman soldiers. This shield was about four feet tall, two feet wide, and, with its curved edges, offered maximum protection. Additionally, when these shields were soaked in water, they were able to extinguish flaming arrows. In the Old Testament, the shield often represented God's protection of his people (see Gen 15:1). The shield of faith protects believers because of their confidence and trust in God and the resources that he provides. Consequently, faith allows us to extinguish "all the flaming darts of the evil one" (6:16). The hostile and destructive attacks by Satan and his minions are thwarted by trust in the God who protects his people.

Stand firm with the helmet of salvation: Again, Paul's language echoes Isaiah 59, where God "put on righteousness as a breastplate" and "a helmet of salvation" (v. 17). Putting on this helmet (which represents salvation) means that we must acknowledge and embrace our new identity in Christ. Because of our union with Christ, we have the power to overcome our enemies.

Stand firm with the sword of the Spirit: This sword, which for a Roman soldier was a short sword designed for close combat, is the Spirit-given word of God. The gospel, the good news of peace and reconciliation through Jesus Christ, is the weapon that believers wield, allowing us to stand firm against our enemies.

REFLECT ON CHRIST

How does the armor of God point us to Christ? First, it is possible that the imagery and language related to the belt of truth alludes to Isaiah 11:4–5, which states, "He shall be girded with righteousness around his waist, and bound with truth around the sides" (NET). The subject of this text is the coming Messiah. If this is the case, then the armor of the righteous and truthful Messiah is now granted to his people. We can stand firm because of the truth of the gospel. Second, the breastplate of righteousness reminds us that fleeing sin and living a holy life is impossible without first experiencing the gift of God's righteousness, which is received through faith in Christ (Rom 3:22). Third, the gospel is described as the "gospel of peace," and earlier in Ephesians, Paul declares that Christ "himself is our peace" (2:14) and that "he came and preached peace" (2:17). It is the gospel of peace because Jesus is the prince of peace who provides peace for his people. Fourth, the helmet of salvation helps us recall that Christ is our Savior, and because of his death and resurrection, our salvation is sure and secured.

APPLY GOD'S WORD

As believers, we are never alone. Not only do we have other Christians who are there to encourage us (either physically with us or as a cloud of faithful witnesses who have gone before us), but God himself is with us. In this passage, Paul emphasizes all three persons of the Trinity in relation to the spiritual battle that surrounds us. God the Father, the divine warrior (see Isa 59:17), offers us his armor and weaponry. We are to take up the full armor of God (6:11, 13), which includes the "word of God" (6:17). God the Son, who defeated death and the devil and is now exalted at the Father's right hand, is the one who strengthens us—"be strong in the Lord" (6:10). Finally, God the Spirit provides us with the sword of the word, and Paul will instruct us to pray "in the Spirit" (6:18).

Do you equip yourself with the armor that God has provided you? This is not something that is done once but something that needs to be done daily. What daily rhythm could you add that would help you employ the full armor of God?

PRAY

O God—Father, Son, Holy Spirit—I am grateful that you have not left me on my own but have provided help in my time of need. Today grant me grace and wisdom to successfully employ your armor to protect me from the enemy and help me advance the good news of Christ. Amen.

STUDY IT FURTHER

1. Study the passages found in Isaiah 11:4–5; 52:7; and 59:17. Do you think these passages provide the background for Paul's armor imagery? Why or why not?

2. Ephesians 6:15 reminds us to have our feet "sandaled with readiness for the gospel of peace" (CSB). Do you think this imagery points primarily to a defensive stance or an offensive stance? Does Isaiah 52:7 help us answer this question?

3. Read John 14:27; 16:33; Romans 5:1; Philippians 4:6–7; and Colossians 3:15, and note the connection between Christ's work and the peace he gives to believers.

Day 39

Ephesians 6:18–20

READ

... praying at all times in the Spirit, with all prayer and supplication. To that end, keep alert with all perseverance, making supplication for all the saints, and also for me, that words may be given to me in opening my mouth boldly to proclaim the mystery of the gospel, for which I am an ambassador in chains, that I may declare it boldly, as I ought to speak.

MEDITATE

Prayer is the focus of this passage, but it is not unrelated to the previous passage that focused on equipping ourselves with the whole armor of God. Prayer is an integral component of standing firm against the enemy. And yet prayer is noticeably distinct from the previous six pieces of armor and weaponry. It is not a seventh piece of armor, since no metaphor is attached to it (e.g., shield of faith). Instead, prayer is foundational for the proper deployment of the armor that God supplies us. Prayer epitomizes what it means to be strong in the Lord (6:10).

The importance of prayer: In verse 18, Paul emphasizes the importance of prayer in at least six ways. First, we are to pray "at all times." In order to effectively stand firm in our faith, we must learn to pray constantly. Twice in Ephesians Paul has demonstrated the centrality of prayer in his own life as he recorded his prayers for the Ephesian believers (1:15–23; 3:14–21). Here, he reminds us to pray continually or at every opportunity. Second, we are to pray "in the Spirit," since it is the Spirit who guides and empowers us. The indwelling Spirit prompts us *to* pray and leads us in *how* to pray and *for whom* to pray. Third, we are to pray "with all prayer and supplication." The repeated use of the terms "prayer" and "supplication" signifies that we should pray diligently and expectantly. Fourth, we are to pray watchfully ("to that end keep alert"). Because the enemy "prowls around like a roaring lion" (1 Pet 5:8), we must stay vigilant and alert. Fifth, we are to pray "with all perseverance." We should not give up on praying. Finally, we are to pray "for all the saints." Because the enemy works best when believers are isolated, we must stand firm by praying for each other.

Specific prayer requests: Paul demonstrates the importance of prayer in his life by asking for specific prayers for himself. First, Paul asks for gospel clarity ("that words may be given to me in the opening of my mouth," 6:19). Paul does not ask for prayer to be released from prison but so that he will faithfully convey the gospel message. Second, he asks for boldness ("boldly to proclaim the mystery of the gospel," 6:19). Because of the seriousness of his situation and the intimidating atmosphere of his imprisonment, he asks for prayer so that he might share the gospel clearly, candidly, and courageously. The repetition of this request ("that I may declare it boldly," 6:20) signifies Paul's desire to declare the good news of Jesus faithfully, even though speaking boldly is what led to his current imprisonment. He reminds his readers that he is "an ambassador in chains" (6:20). The irony here is ambassadors were typically given special privileges, which often included immunity from imprisonment. For Paul, the overwhelming compulsion to share the gospel relates to his divine calling and is therefore something he "ought to speak" (6:20).

REFLECT ON CHRIST

At least two components of this passage draw our attention to Christ. First, Paul asks for prayer that he would boldly proclaim "the mystery of the gospel" (6:19). As we have seen before in Ephesians, the mystery of which Paul speaks is the gospel. More specifically, it is the revelation that Jews and gentiles have become the one people of God through their common faith and union with Jesus Christ. The message that Paul was willing to risk his own life for centered on Jesus. He asks for continued courage to faithfully proclaim the message of the gospel of Jesus Christ. Second, Paul calls himself "an ambassador in chains" (6:20). In 2 Corinthians 5:20, Paul writes, "Therefore, we are ambassadors for Christ, God making his appeal through us. We implore you on behalf of Christ, be reconciled to God." Paul did not preach himself but Jesus Christ and him crucified (1 Cor 1:23; 2:2). He was a representative of God given the commission to reveal the mystery of the gospel. He spoke with the authority of another proclaiming the message of the King.

APPLY GOD'S WORD

In the last passage, I suggested that some of the imagery Paul uses does not merely convey a defensive posture but how believers can actively advance the gospel (especially the shoes that signify "the readiness given by the gospel of peace" [6:15] and the "sword of the Spirit" [6:17]). This attacking, offense-oriented posture is then modeled by Paul, who asks for prayer that he might boldly preach the gospel. Prayer becomes a powerful weapon that helps us advance the light of the gospel into the darkness. When we faithfully pray, we are able to stand firm against the schemes of the devil and boldly proclaim the gospel. But without prayer, the armor and weapons needed for battle are often not effectively or successfully employed.

What would it look like in your life to pray "at all times," "with all prayer and supplication," "with all perseverance," and "for all the saints" (6:18)? Clearly Paul is stressing the need and importance for prayer as we press on, seeking to advance the gospel. What is at least one element related to prayer that you could add to help you pray as Paul instructs us in Ephesians 6?

PRAY

God, help me to pray at all times, to pray in the Spirit, to pray with all prayer and supplication, to pray with alertness, to pray with all perseverance, and to pray for all the saints. Help me boldly to proclaim the mystery of the gospel as your ambassador. Amen.

STUDY IT FURTHER

1. Paul urges us to pray "at all times." Read Acts 1:14; 2:42; and 6:4 to see the importance of prayer in the early church. Also see Romans 12:12; Colossians 4:2; and 1 Thessalonians 5:17, where Paul similarly encourages us to pray steadfastly. Is prayer part of your daily rhythm? If not, how could it become part of it?

2. Paul often included prayer requests in his letters (see Rom 15:30–32; 2 Cor 1:11; Col 4:3–4; 1 Thess 5:25; 2 Thess 3:1–2).

How might it encourage us to be willing to request prayer if the apostle Paul was willing to do so?

3. In 2 Timothy 4:17, Paul writes, "But the Lord stood by me and strengthened me, so that through me the message might be fully proclaimed and all the Gentiles might hear it." Could this be an answer to Paul's prayer request in Ephesians 6:19–20?

Day 40

Ephesians 6:21–24

READ

So that you also may know how I am
and what I am doing, Tychicus the beloved brother
and faithful minister in the Lord will tell you everything.
I have sent him to you for this very purpose, that you may
know how we are, and that he may encourage
your hearts. Peace be to the brothers, and love with faith,
from God the Father and the Lord Jesus Christ.
Grace be with all who love
our Lord Jesus Christ with love incorruptible.

MEDITATE

After writing a somewhat lengthy letter that provides his readers with both theological and practical instruction, Paul concludes with a commendation of Tychicus and with a short prayer and benediction.

Knowing and encouraging others: Paul often includes personal information at the end of his letters. In Ephesians, his brief comments focus on Tychicus, who was probably the letter's courier. Tychicus was one of Paul's most trusted coworkers, and here Paul refers to him as a "beloved brother" and a "faithful minister" (6:21). It is likely that he carried and delivered not only the letter of Ephesians but also Colossians, Philemon, 2 Timothy, and Titus. Paul had two purposes for mentioning Tychicus. First, Tychicus was sent to provide the Ephesians with additional information regarding Paul's situation (6:21, 22). Tychicus had the responsibility of relaying first-hand information about Paul's situation in prison. Second, he was sent to encourage the hearts of the Ephesians (6:22). Most likely, these two reasons are related, because once they knew about Paul's situation (his health, the nature of his imprisonment, and how God was working through Paul even in his imprisonment), they would have been encouraged. Knowledge about Paul's current situation led to encouragement. Paul's goal was to encourage his readers by updating them with knowledge about his circumstances.

Blessing others: After encouraging his readers, Paul offers a brief prayer and benediction. Paul's prayer focuses on peace, love, and faith: "Peace be to the brothers, and love with faith, from God the Father and the Lord Jesus Christ" (6:23). "Peace" was a common term used in prayers and benedictions, and its place at the beginning of this prayer demonstrates its prominence. "Love" and "faith" have also been significant themes throughout the letter of Ephesians. Paul's benediction also focuses on grace: "Grace be with all who love our Lord Jesus Christ with love incorruptible" (6:24). Grace is given to those who have a personal relationship with the Lord Jesus Christ. Paul describes the love we have for Jesus as "incorruptible," signifying a persistent or undying love. Because our love is not diminished or affected by death, it will continue unceasingly and endlessly. This type of love is only possible because of the love we first experience from God: "We love because he first loved us" (1 John 4:19).

REFLECT ON CHRIST

Even in Paul's final greeting, Christ is prominent. First, Tychicus is described as a beloved and faithful servant "in the Lord" (6:21). All of our service and work in the gospel is *because of* Jesus and *for* Jesus. Second, the peace that we receive, along with the love and faith, comes to us not only from God the Father but from "the Lord Jesus Christ" (6:23). Jesus, the Second Person of the Trinity, blesses us with peace, love, and faith. Third, grace is given to those who specifically love "the Lord Jesus Christ" (6:24). The grace that we receive is dependent on our relationship with Jesus. Those who do not love him do not receive this grace, whereas those who do love him receive this grace. Grace, God's saving grace in particular, flows to those who have been renewed and who love his Son.

APPLY GOD'S WORD

Paul was not a lone Christian who served God in isolation. This concluding passage gives us a glimpse into Paul's life and ministry, revealing how he partnered with and was dependent on others. Paul always served on a team. Whenever he traveled, planted, or strengthened churches, or even when he was in prison, he relied on and worked together with others. Along with investing in and partnering with others like Tychicus, Paul sought to encourage fellow believers, even when he was the one who was in need of encouragement. Writing from prison, Paul sent a letter to the believers in Ephesus to instruct, exhort, and to encourage them in their walk. He also prayed for them, wishing God's blessings of peace, love, faith, and grace in their lives. Just as he began this letter with an extended praise to God for granting his people every spiritual blessing, he now ends the letter with a prayer and benediction of blessing. Instead of being consumed with his own grim circumstances as a prisoner of Rome, he considered others as more significant than himself (see Phil 2:3–4).

Is there someone in your life who could use encouragement from you? What could you do to encourage them? Perhaps you could write them a letter, email, or text or call them. Are you in the habit of praying God's blessings in the lives of others? Paul doesn't pray for their health or wealth but for them to receive God's peace, love, and grace. Pray for these blessings today for someone you know.

PRAY

God, thank you that I have received your peace, love, and grace. Help me to be an encouragement to others today so that others can share in these blessings.
Burden my heart with the needs of others so that I am more concerned with their well-being than my own. Amen.

STUDY IT FURTHER

1. Tychicus was Paul's faithful and trusted coworker. Read Acts 20:4; Colossians 4:7–9; 2 Timothy 4:12; and Titus 3:12 to see where he is referenced elsewhere in relation to Paul and his ministry.

2. In Ephesians 6:23–24, Paul prays for God's "peace," "love," and "grace" in the lives of his readers. Each one of these terms has been highlighted throughout the book of Ephesians (for peace, see 2:14–18; 4:3; 6:15; for love, see 2:4; 3:14–19; 5:1–2; for grace, see 1:6, 7; 2:5, 7, 8; 4:7).Pray

for peace, love, and grace for others in your life, bringing in elements of the other verses that reference these terms in Ephesians.

3. The believer's relationship with Christ is characterized by love ("all who love our Lord Jesus Christ," 6:24). Read the following passages to see where love is emphasized in that relationship (Exod 20:6; Deut 5:10; 7:9; Rom 8:28; 1 Cor 2:9; 8:3; Jas 1:12; 2:5). How have you been marked by Christ's love for you?

Group Reading Plan

What follows is a suggested plan for reading through this study in a group, with six days of study per week.

WEEK 1

1. Introduction to Ephesians
2. Ephesians 1:1–2
3. Ephesians 1:3–6
4. Ephesians 1:7–10
5. Ephesians 1:11–12
6. Ephesians 1:13–14

WEEK 2

1. Ephesians 1:15–17
2. Ephesians 1:18–23
3. Ephesians 2:1–3
4. Ephesians 2:4
5. Ephesians 2:5–7
6. Ephesians 2:8–10

WEEK 3

1. Ephesians 2:11–13
2. Ephesians 2:14–18
3. Ephesians 2:19–22
4. Ephesians 3:1–7
5. Ephesians 3:8–13
6. Ephesians 3:14–19

WEEK 4

1. Ephesians 3:20–21
2. Ephesians 4:1–3
3. Ephesians 4:4–6
4. Ephesians 4:7–10
5. Ephesians 4:11–12
6. Ephesians 4:13–16

WEEK 5

1. Ephesians 4:17–19
2. Ephesians 4:20–24
3. Ephesians 4:25–32
4. Ephesians 5:1–2
5. Ephesians 5:3–6
6. Ephesians 5:7–14

WEEK 6

1. Ephesians 5:15–17
2. Ephesians 5:18–21
3. Ephesians 5:22–24
4. Ephesians 5:25–33
5. Ephesians 6:1–4
6. Ephesians 6:5–9

WEEK 7

1. Ephesians 6:10
2. Ephesians 6:11–13
3. Ephesians 6:14–17
4. Ephesians 6:18–20
5. Ephesians 6:21–24